INNOVATIVE ARCHITECTURE
OF SINGAPORE

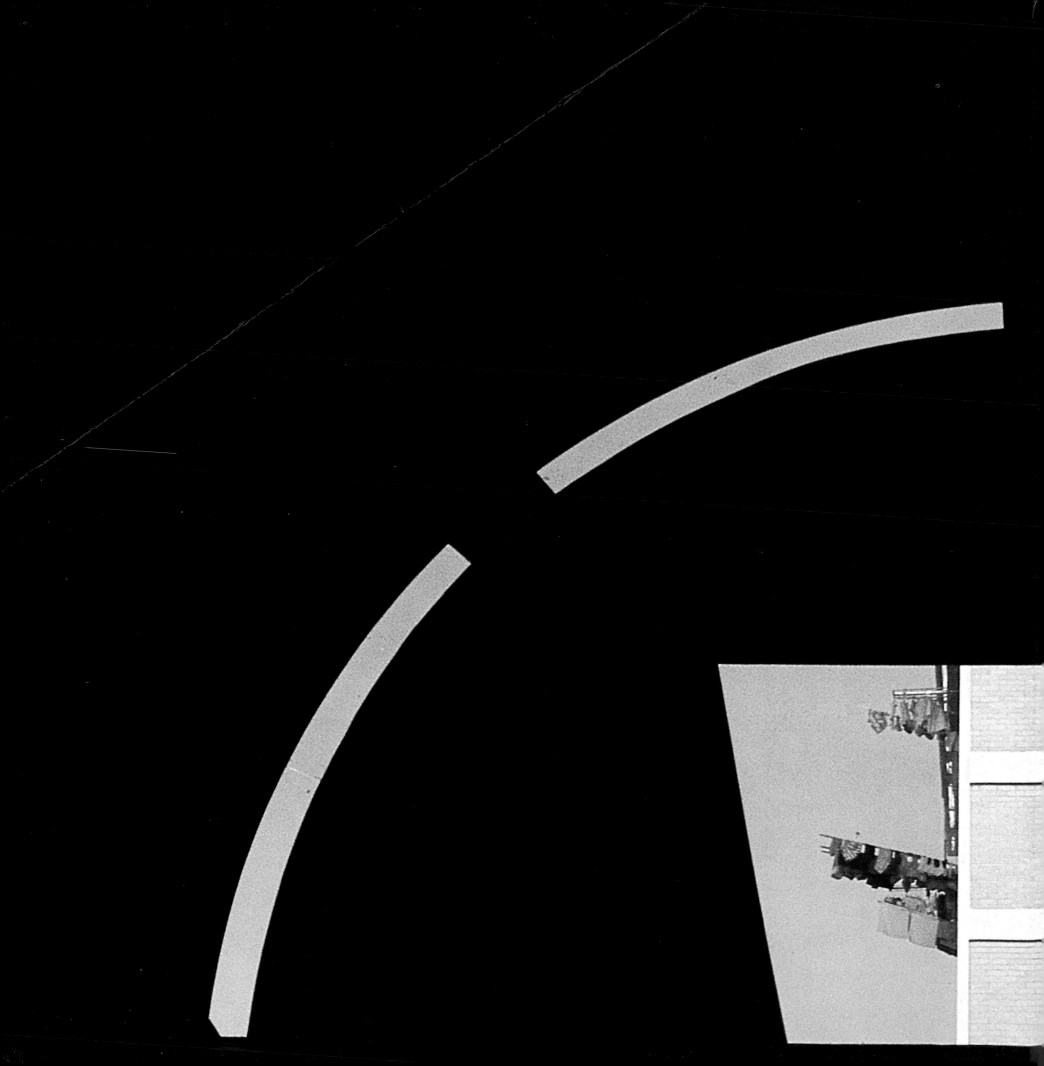

INNOVATIVE ARCHITECTURE
OF SINGAPORE

Robert Powell
Foreword by Charles Correa

SELECT BOOKS

Photography: Albert Lim K.S.

© Select Books Pte Ltd & Select Management Pte Ltd

Published by
SELECT BOOKS PTE LTD
19, Tanglin Road, #03-15,
Singapore 1024

Produced and Designed by
LANDMARK BOOKS PTE LTD
5001, Beach Road, 02-73/74, Singapore 0719

ISBN 981-00-0683-7

Typeset at Superskill Graphics Pte Ltd
Colour Separations by Eray Scan Pte Ltd
Printed by Times Litho Pte Ltd

ACKNOWLEDGEMENTS

The seeds of the idea for this book on innovative architecture of Singapore took root in early 1987 when I was fortunate to meet Lena Lim U Wen of Select Books. Her enthusiastic response at our first meeting and subsequent commitment to the book opened the way to an excellent collaboration.

We courted Goh Eck Kheng of Landmark Books who had just produced a centenary publication for the National Museum and great was our delight when he expressed an interest in handling the design and production.

The team was completed when Eck Kheng introduced Albert Lim K.S. who is responsible for the excellent photographs in this book.

The eminent Indian Architect Charles Correa agreed to write a Foreword to place Singapore's architecture in the global context, specifically, its relation to other parts of Asia.

I am indebted to Lynda Lim who typed the texts of my previous three books and this one too.

Nirmal Kishnani, now an architect with the Public Works Department, assisted me immediately after his graduation, in the documentation of buildings for inclusion while Kevin Lim Siew Teck, before commencing his post graduate studies, photographed all of the buildings for my reference. The plans of all projects have been redrawn by Dennis Chan. I am grateful to them.

I must thank a number of undergraduates whose perceptive comments and essays on contemporary buildings added to my first hand observations. Sometimes they were able to give an entirely different perspective. I would specifically mention Tan Hock Beng, Wong Mun Summ, Raymond Teo, Siew Man Kok, Peter Cheng, Maria Hartarti, Rajmah bte Taib, Daniel Wong, Loo Kok Hoo and Leong Howe Ngai. Some of their comments have been quoted within the pages of this book.

My thanks to the architects who have assisted me with information. I hope that where I have repaid their kindness by being critical of their designs, they will accept that the critique is but my opinion and see criticism as a positive part of the creative process. Similarly, I appreciate the generosity of the building owners in allowing access. Innovative architecture it has to be stressed, requires a meeting of minds between architect and client.

My particular thanks for the insights provided in conversations with Charles Correa and Tay Kheng Soon as well as the ideas articulated by Bobby Wong Chong Thai. The support of William Lim and Norman Edwards has been invaluable, while others have helped in ways they are probably not aware of.

Lastly to Shantheni for her love and support.

CONTENTS

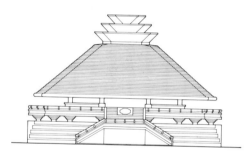

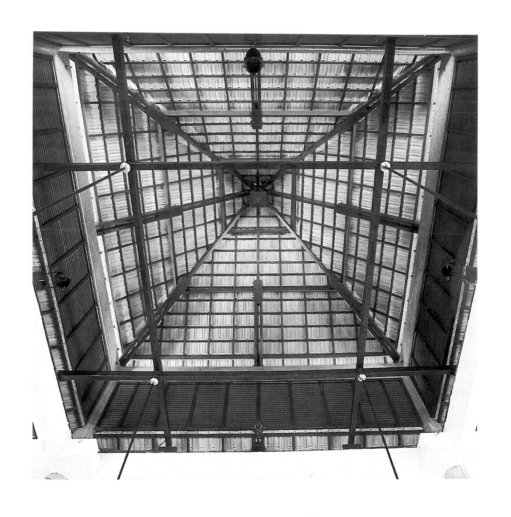

FOREWORD

Architecture goes beyond pragmatic considerations and superficial formalism in order to re-invent the mythic images and values which lie in the deep-structure of our subconscious.

This has always been true of the work of the best architects even in this century. For instance, whether one likes Corbusier's buildings or not, all of them have clearly the stamp of *un homme Mediterranée*; yet none of them uses a sloping roof of red tiles. Instead, Corbusier seems to have taken the age-old images and values of the Mediterranean and (perhaps unconsciously? compulsively?) re-invented them within the 20th century technology of concrete and glass. This is true transformation. It places Architecture where it rightfully belongs: at the intersection of culture, technology and aspiration.

Whenever we build, as Louis Sullivan has pointed out, we reveal something about ourselves. In this sense Architecture is an extraordinarily sensitive indicator of our times, of our values and of our dreams. Like a snail secreting its own habitat as it inches forward, every society is constantly (and perhaps blindly) expressing itself — and in the process creating the environment that will condition the next generation. ("We build our buildings and then our buildings build us"). In this process, human aspirations are of crucial importance. Consider, for instance, the truly extraordinary houses created around the turn of the century in the mid-western states of the U.S.A. by Frank Lloyd Wright. It would seem that in that oeuvre, Wright single-handedly invented the way the American middle-class was going to live. The builders' houses constructed in suburbia over the last three or four decades are really just hand-me-down versions of Wright's Usonian prototypes, with all the mythic imagery intact: the two steps up to the raised dining area, the carport, the picture window, and so forth. How did Wright do it? Not because of any dependence on historic "quotes" or "reference" (surely architects who study only History are condemned to repeat it?) but because he understood well the culture and technology of his times, and most important of all — because he could read perfectly the aspirations of the middle Americans he was addressing.

What are the aspirations of Singapore today? In order to find the answer we must understand a concept which has dominated most of this century, and which is quite out-of-fashion today: the *tabla rasa*. This concept of a clean slate has profound advantages and disadvantages. On the negative side, the denial of any umbilical cord handicaps the creation of meaningful cultural gestures. On the other hand, addressing life without any preconceptions has crucial advantages as well: Singapore is much more than just another economic miracle; it is one of the few countries in this part of the world where the various communities (Chinese, Malay, Indian, European, etc) live together in harmony. In an Asia racked by caste prejudice, clan loyalties, and just old-fashioned bigotry, this is achievement indeed.

In such a context, how can Architecture help generate the roots that society seek? This is the issue that this book addresses. And in it, we can perceive the documentation of an extraordinary moment in history — a moment in which Singapore (an Asian society both very young and very old) is setting out on the task of defining its identity.

Many years ago, returning as a student by boat to India, I heard a fellow-passenger, a Pakistani, play the piano beautifully. She had studied western classical music at Julliard, and just before leaving America, she had asked her teacher: "I wonder what I will do when I get back home — there aren't any really good teachers in Karachi". Her teacher had replied: "At your stage, you don't need good teachers... you need good listeners."

That is the heart of our predicament in this part of the world: the lack of good listeners. Too often, talent in India atrophies not due to Failure but, ironically enough, due to its own success. An indifferent film by Satyajit Ray can illicit the same enthusiastic response as was accorded his breathtaking masterpiece Pather Panchali. Without the discriminating listener, the artist is denied the feed-back loop so essential to the nourishment of his talent — and of art.

Robert Powell is a good listener. The clarity, sensitivity and honesty of his perceptions have made a unique contribution not only to the School of Architecture at the National University of Singapore where he teaches, but to the profession at large in the region of Southeast Asia. With this book, he starts a process of listening which is going to be of crucial importance to the development of architecture in this part of the world.

Charles Correa
January 1989

9

INTRODUCTION

Singapore has always been a melting pot of races and architectural influences. The first Hongkong and Shanghai Bank, attributed to Swan and MacLaren (built in 1892 and demolished in 1919), reflected an earlier period of rapid transition in Singapore's history.

Every society in the so-called 'developing world' in the late 1980s is part of a discourse which sees the movement away from universal absolute values towards a regional view. This book is a mirror held up to that rhetoric and looks at its reflection in the light of the architecture of Singapore.

There is now an ideological shift away from universalism which has many dimensions — political, social, economic and anthropological. This is in concord with the theory of architect and historian J.R. Lethaby, who noted that 'developments of building practice mirror the general development of world ideas'.[1]

The most succinct summary of the dilemma which confronts nations rising from underdevelopment is by the French philosopher Paul Ricouer.[2] 'In order to get on the road to modernisation, is it necessary to jettison the old cultural past? ... On the one hand the nation has to root itself in the soil of its past, forge a national spirit and unfurl this spiritual and cultural revindication of the colonialists personality. But in order to take part in modern civilisation, it is necessary at the same time to take part in scientific, technical and political rationality; something which often requires the pure and simple abandonment of a whole cultural past. There is the paradox; how to become modern and to return to your sources.'

This situation is not peculiar to Singapore or even to South-east Asia. In 1987, the Prime Minister of Malta

speaking on the same phenomena in the context of the Meditteranean region, noted that 'A strong awareness of the local and regional identity is a most useful quality to have in the political situation of the world in the 1980s. It allows a country to remain open to foreign influences without much danger that its native traditions will be submerged. It allows a society to assimiliate modern technology without the submersion of its ethos and values. It allows a culture to grow and develop by responding to stimulae and challenges coming from outside without losing its soul in the process.'[3]

It is a theme which Prime Minister Lee Kuan Yew took up in August 1988. In a forum on 'Changes in Singapore', he told university students that all-permeating Western influence could well mean the erosion of Asian qualities. "It is a problem," he is quoted as saying. "We are under assault." Indeed he went on to say that "Singapore was in danger of becoming a pseudo-Western society because of the English language school system."[4]

Contemporary architecture, like language, can be seen against this global discourse. Brig-Gen Lee Hsien Loong, Singapore's Minister for Trade and Industry, speaking to Singaporean Chinese newspaper editors in July 1988 reminded them that, "The challenge facing Singapore is how to retain the cultural and social values that come with the Chinese language as English becomes even more dominant as

the working language. Whether Singaporeans can survive as a nation in South-east Asia depends on their ability to retain traditional values and keep them as relevant and 'living parts' of their heritage in the face of change".[5]

Brig-Gen Lee returned to this theme a month later when he was commenting on a proposal by First Deputy Prime Minister Goh Chok Tong, that the government should formulate a national ideology to keep their Asian bearings as Singapore progresses into the 21st Century. "A national ideology," he said, "is a very serious requirement for a constantly changing society that has already become more Westernised from the exposure to all things foreign."[6]

The paradox is that in the same week, Singapore hosted a conference on Global Strategies aimed at finding out the thinking of Multi-National Corporations and how Singapore can play a more prominent role in international business.

There is thus a tug-of-war between internationalism and regionalism, modernism and traditionalism, technology and craft skills.

Singapore is at the cutting edge of this discourse and any book on contemporary Singapore architecture must locate innovative design in 'the current of international, national and regional debate.'[7]

BACKGROUND

If Singapore's architecture can be seen as part of this global dialogue

between universalism and regionalism, it must even more so be a reflection of Singapore's socio-political and intellectual milieu. "We are going through," to quote architect Tay Kheng Soon, "the most interesting phase of South-east Asian cultural history. We are doing so during a period of questioning of the modernisation process itself, and the awakening of cultural consciousness everywhere. Most of the architects in Singapore (and Malaysia) have been trained abroad and, with the emergence of the new cultural imperatives, must undoubtedly be questioning themselves regarding their ideas and their role."[8]

Singapore became an independent state in 1965. The government initiated tough legislation to acquire land and properties for public purposes. The aim was to create a favourable investment climate and to build up the island's potential as an *entrepôt* port. The Government's Home Ownership Scheme, introduced in 1964 has succeeded in creating, through the Housing and Development Board (HDB), large numbers of reasonably-priced housing units. This achievement has been accompanied by major urban renewal and the establishment of new towns.[9] Several United Nations reports in the early 1960s formed the basis of government planning. Slum clearance and urban renewal were considered to be of the highest priority according to a paper by Alan FC Choe in 1968.[10] The emphasis was placed on a pragmatic approach to the renewal of the urban core and

thus, the demolition of large numbers of buildings of architectural and historical interest was considered an acceptable and fair price to pay for 'progress'.

There were many heated debates in the late 1960s about the impact of changing values, and the government response to those changes. Architect William SW Lim, writing of the period, has noted that, 'Many young local architects, inspired by the spirit of the time and heightened sense of national consciousness, made serious attempts to reinterpret the role of architecture and its development to suit local conditions. Whenever opportunities were available, attempts were made to design culturally and climatic responsive projects from houses to educational buildings, hotels to shopping centres. Many heated discussions and ideas were generated to evaluate the impact of changing values, life styles and social conditions on the total urban environment. The architectural quality of

the buildings may vary, but the intellectual commitment and energy generated by these architects was unmistakeable: many of the ideas were very idealistic and considered unfavourably by the authorities. It was an interesting and creative period".[11]

1964 saw the emergence of the Singapore Planning and Urban Research Group (SPUR), a multi-disciplinary society of professionals, academics and businessmen concerned with, and about, the urban environment. Committed to an intellectual search for urban solutions, the exchange of ideas and public discussion, it eschewed alignment with any political party. The members of SPUR questioned conventional wisdom on many issues which occasionally brought them into conflict with the government. The group dissolved in the 1970s.

Positions adopted on urban development issues became entrenched. Rigid demarcation between the work of the public authority archi-

The Housing and Development Board has since its formation, succeeded in creating a large number of reasonably priced housing units. Four out of every five Singaporeans live in a HDB apartment. The achievements of the HDB are chronicled in the book *Designed for Living* (1985). Public Housing is, for many visitors, the predominant architectural image of Singapore.

11

Habitat (1984, with additions in 1986) is Singapore's version of the first Habitat building constructed as part of the Montreal Expo '67 by Moshe Safdie. The Singapore design is by the architect in association with Regional Development Consortium. It is a controlled geometric composition which influenced RDC's design for Balestier Point (p. 64).

tect and private practitioners became the norm. This segregation of architectural professionals led to a public sector workload which was seven times the volume of that undertaken by architects in private practice.

These worlds of the government architect and of the private practitioner have existed separately until recently in Singapore. Each has been almost totally insulated from the other. Such a situation prevented the development of a diversity of design approaches. 'Ideas from outside of sanctioned quarters have been rare and independent ideas largely untapped and diffused.'[12]

Each sector is only now, according to Tay Kheng Soon, becoming aware of the potential of the other. 'This new understanding is recent; since the Singapore Government's Economic Committee's efforts to cope with the 1987 recession. It was shown how new conceptual windows were more quickly opened through a healthy exchange of honest ideas.'[13]

The imbalance between the amount of work done by the Government and the private architect in the last twenty years has meant the shape of the city and its predominant architectural image has been generated by one single agency.

'The result is the conventionalisation of design ideas ... there is a need to produce uniform results so as not to be accused of being unfair. In housing this is especially so. This process, of course, acts against experimentation and innovation ... which is why differences in housing are cosmetic with surface stylistic differences only.'[14]

Looking back over 25 years, this single agency's response is that Singapore is 'a long way ahead of cities and countries where citizens struggle for roofs over their heads, or where water and electricity supplies, sewer and drainage systems are privileged accessories.'[15]

From an original brief to relieve the urgent housing problems in the early 1960s, the HDB has, to date, provided accommodation for four out of five Singaporeans — a proud record. The HDB acknowledged that there are shortcomings and that no government would voluntarily opt for high-rise, high density living, but that it was the only viable choice. Under its Chief Executive, Liu Thai Ker, the HDB has now turned its attention to the question of giving estates distinct character and identity, seeking inspiration from local, tropical and regional forms.[16]

The early critics of the choice of high-rise concede that the HDB's achievements are remarkable even if it has been achieved by resorting to a high degree of standardisation in design. To quote William SW Lim, 'The Planning ideas and architectural style of the housing authority are firmly based on the theoretical and aesthetic framework of the Modern Movement.'[17]

By any standards, the public housing estates are well managed and planned with comprehensive support facilities. There are playgrounds for children and a wide variety of shops in each town centre. Vandalism is low and the only possible problem that looms on the horizon for future Town Councils is the rising cost of maintenance.

The OCBC Centre (1975). Designed by I M Pei and Partners in association with BEP Akitek, the building is a powerful statement of corporate power. It is the headquarters of the Overseas Chinese Banking Corporation. Some observers see, in its architectural form, a representation of a giant calculator; others the Chinese character for the surname of its creator, I M Pei. It is an interesting example of 'meaning' conveyed by architecture.

INFLUENCE OF FOREIGN ARCHITECTS

The architecture of the city has, since the mid-1970s, been dominated by foreign architects. Given opportunities by both public and private decision makers, Moshe Safdie, IM Pei, Kenzo Tange, John Portman, Paul Rudolph, among others, have introduced buildings in association with local practices.

Part of the reason for this influx of famous names was the Land Sales policy introduced as part of a strategy for the comprehensive redevelopment of the central area.

This resulted in a scramble for the rich profits to be made in developing large sites in prominent locations. Proposals and schemes were submitted and a key factor in winning bids appears to have been the choice of internationally recognised 'names' to do the design, albeit in association with a local practice.

Some of the resulting buildings are fine examples of modern architecture which match the best in the world. The OCBC Centre, the result of the Second Sale of Sites in 1968, designed by IM Pei and Partners in association with BEP Akitek, is one such building. To quote the architects, 'The Overseas Chinese Banking Corporation Centre exudes a sense of strength and permenance'. It is also, to quote Edwards and Keys, 'an exceedingly forceful statement of megastructural power'.[18]

John Portman and Associates, in association with DP Architects, are responsible for Marina Square — the hotel, shopping and entertainment complex which is based on North American models. It is the largest development of its kind in Southeast Asia with three international hotels all utilising the Portman trademark — the internal atrium first developed in his Peachtree development in Atlanta, USA.

John Portman was responsible for another version of his atrium design, the Pavilion Inter-Continental (renamed the Regent in 1988), in association with BEP Akitek. Completed in 1982, it was his first hotel design outside the USA.

There are others: Raffles City by IM Pei in association with Architects 61, the OUB Centre by Kenzo Tange with SAA Partnership, and Mosche Safdie's Habitat in association with Regional Development Consortium, to name just three.

The nation's wish to express progress and modernity is reflected in these international symbols of modern corporate architecture. They are, by any criteria, well designed and constructed buildings.

However, there are those who would argue that good as they are, the basic impulse for *innovative* architecture has to come from those committed to the internal dynamics of the country. 'The large scale introduction of International Style buildings,' comments William Lim, 'may provide a superficial image of progress and modernity. However it often destroys the fragile experiment in the evolutionary development of localism and identity.'[20]

This point has been echoed by

14

Singapore, an Asian society which is both very young and very old, is searching for an architectural language that seeks to synthesise Modernity and Tradition, Internationalism and Regionalism, High Technology and Craft Skills.

The Singapore skyline depicts the dialectic between these polarities.

Alongside the shophouses on Boat Quay are the towering commercial buildings, many by foreign consultants. In the foreground is the heart of colonial Singapore. To the right, in the background, are early high-rise apartments by the Housing and Development Board.

The challenge facing the present generation of Singaporean architects is to create a tropical (regional) modern architecture.

Singapore Rubber House (1960). By Swan and Mclaren, the appearance of the building is very much that of the post-war international style. Concrete brise-soleil are used as a response to sunlight, in the manner of Corbusier at Chandigarh. Jane Drew, one of Corbusier's collaborators on the design for the Punjab capital, designed the interiors of Rubber House.

Tay Kheng Soon. 'To raise national consciousness through design needs a conceptual breakthrough. Foreign expertise has not broken any new ground. No new design issue or themes intrinsic to Singapore have emerged. Moreover, the designs are conceptually conventional and conservative. They have not addressed any Singapore issues.'[21]

In short, innovation has and will come about with new concepts and innovation from local architects, and not from transplanted models.

NEW DIRECTIONS

It is against this background that innovation in architecture is considered. *Innovative Architecture of Singapore* is a title that will generate mixed reactions. As Singaporeans arguably move into the phase of 'self-actualisation', described in Maslow's theory of human development, the debate about architecture must reflect the values of a society in rapid transition. The new emphasis on creativity and research-led initiatives suggests that 'when we discuss excellence in the built environment, we need to step back and view the sweep of events that have happened and the momentus changes taking place now.'[22]

These changes are also happening in other parts of the world, where many of the ruling elites have gone through a process of dissociation from their cultural roots. This has led, according to a Director of the World Bank, Ismail Serageldin, to a 'dichotomisation' of cultural perception 'where the historical heritage, cultural, religious, spiritual, is identified with the past as backwardness and poverty, while the image of "progress" in the future is borrowed from elsewhere, namely the West. The problem created by the externally borrowed image of progress is very severe.

It poses a challenge for architects who have to articulate a vision for the future which is culturally authentic and yet incorporates all the progressive elements that societies in transition aspire towards.'[23]

Serageldin delves into this problem and concludes that 'architects must acquire a level of sophistication in their ability to read the symbolic context of their heritage in a manner that enriches their ability to produce relevant buildings for today ... The architect's role is pivotal in societies in transition, in defining society's sense of its own reality.'[24]

How is this reflected in Singapore's architecture? The buildings illustrated between these covers show the growing confidence and innovative ability of a generation of architects since independence. Most of the buildings have been completed in the half decade between 1983 and 1988. They indicate several strands of innovation, but all are in one way or another a response to imperatives of climate or culture.

There is no 'style' of architecture here. Though they do not easily fit together, there is an eclectic freshness about them, and they indicate a move away from the uniform, regular, economic, assembly line production, and stereotyped buildings which were reflective of social and political values of the 1960s and 1970s. The buildings of that period were recognisable as 'industrially rational forms, big blank blocks, functional, treated non-essentially and finite, closed forms which cannot be easily modified.'[25]

The changing social values of the latter half of the 1980s bring a questioning of Western values, references to the plural cultural roots

Bank of China (1953-1954). Designed by Palmer and Turner, this building was one of the region's first high-rise tower blocks, though modest (18 storeys) by comparison with many later giants. It was a forerunner of the technology packed office blocks of today as it was Singapore's first centrally air-conditioned skyscraper. There is an interesting duality between the modern classical facades and the use of Chinese details in stone and bronze.

of Singapore and an increasingly strong conservation movement which contrasts sharply with the mood at the beginning of the decade. At the same time, in reaction to the architectural idioms of the recent past, there are increasingly variagated forms of housing and a degree of humour in design.

The buildings in this book exhibit some of these characteristics; a hybrid of change, continuity and conservation. They also satisfy an important aspect of architecture; they are not simply functional and efficient buildings, indeed some may have critics on these grounds, but architecture is an *art*, and all the buildings illustrated give much visual delight.

THE ROOTS OF INNOVATION

Innovation in the architecture of Singapore did not appear suddenly in the mid 1980s. The strong roots of innovative architecture in the private sector can be traced at least as far back as the late 1950s. Several practices were prominent in postwar colonial Singapore, amongst them Palmer and Turner which had offices in Hong Kong and also in Shanghai up to the outbreak of the Second World War. Others such as Swan and Mclaren, Raglan Squires Partnership and Booty Edwards and Partners were well established, as was James Ferrie who set up his own practice in 1953 on leaving Palmer and Turner.

The post war period, to quote Seow Eu Jin , brought 'a young gen-

Asia Insurance Building (1954). Ng Kheng Siang was the first Singaporean to become a member of the Royal Institute of British Architects. In the mid-1950s, this was the tallest building in Singapore and it is arguably the first attempt to produce a building of Modern Regional architecture.

18

eration of Singaporean architects trained in Australia, England, Canada and the United States as well as in the local architectural school ... whose heroes ranged from Le Corbusier, Gropius, Mies, Neutra, Breur and Kahn ... to Maekawa, Tange, Kurokawa and Pei.'[26]

Ng Kheng Siang had a huge practice in the 1950s with a wide spectrum of work. His most lasting project, still a beautiful landmark in down-town Singapore today is the Asia Building completed in 1954. It was as innovative in its time as any building in this book.

Seow Eu Jin himself was a leading architect in this same period, and several returning graduates worked with him in the practice of Seow, Lee, Heah and Partners. Cambridge educated CAV Chew was one; he later went on to become a partner of Kumpulan Akitek a practice that was founded as early as 1957 under the style of CAV Chew and Partners, but adopted its present name in 1964. Tan Cheng Siong, a Singapore Polytechnic graduate, also started his career with Seow, Lee, Heah and Partners, leaving in 1967 to become a partner in Archynamics Architects.

'Archynamics were the "star" architects of the time.'[27] When the practice dissolved in 1974, two partners, Chan Fook Pong and Kenneth Chen Koon Lap, formed Regional Development Consortium (RDC) Architects whilst Tan Cheng Siong set up Archurban Architects Planners — a practice credited with the

highly original Pandan Valley Condominium Housing Development.

Timothy Seow, educated at Oxford joined Scow, Lee, Heah and Partners and on the retirement of the firm's founder Dr Seow Eu Jin in 1974, formed his own practice Timothy Seow and Partners. The Futura Apartments on Leonie Hill, completed in 1976 to Seow's design, was a dynamic vision of the future.

Another prominent architect of post-war Singapore is Alfred Wong who established Alfred Wong and Partners in 1957. His 'constant originality in design'[28] was revealed in several churches, also this same originality is evident in the Marco Polo Hotel completed in 1968.

Another strong tap root of innovation has to be mentioned. Lim Chong Keat, a young graduate of Manchester University and MIT, worked briefly with Seow Eu Jin after graduation, and in 1960, he formed with Chen Voon Fee and William SW Lim the practice of Malayan Architects Co-Partnership. William SW Lim had previously worked for three years with James Ferrie after graduating from the Architectural Association and Harvard. The practice of Malayan Architects Co-Partnership was highly innovative and when it was dissolved, it spawned a number of today's most influential firms.

On the dissolution of Malayan Architects Co-Partnership, Lim Chong Keat set up Architects Team 3 in 1967, retiring from the Singapore firm in December 1980, and

Pandan Valley Condominium (1976-1979). This condominium development by Archurban Architects Planners is an early and innovative example of this now common building type. It is particularly noteworthy for its sensitive use of the topography

Marco Polo Hotel (1968, with extensions in 1981). Originally known as Hotel Malaysia and now Omni Marco Polo, the building was designed by the Alfred Wong Partnership.

becoming a partner of Team 3 International. Chen Voon Fee worked out of Kuala Lumpur whilst William SW Lim, along with Koh Seow Chuan and Tay Kheng Soon (both associates of Malayan Architects Co-Partnership at the time of its dissolution) were founding partners of Design Partnership.

In 1975, Tay Kheng Soon left Design Partnership to form Akitek Tenggara and in the same year, Design Partnership reformed as DP Architects. In 1981, William Lim retired from DP Architects and set up the new practice of William Lim Associates, whilst DP Architects consolidated under its present partners, Koh Seow Chuan, Gan Eng Oon and Chan Sui Him.

These then, are the rich sources of innovation which find expression today. In addition, a number of long-time residents have added their contribution. These include Geoffrey Malone and Philip Conn of International Project Consultants, Ian Lander and Gordon Benton, the latter two having been with the long established James Ferrie Partnership. Added to these are Manop Phakinsri, Sompolpong Boonchai and Paul Tsakok — architects who established practices in Singapore. Tsakok and Manop Phakinsri both joined Design Partnership when they first came to Singapore before later branching out on their own. Recently formed practices such as TangGuanBee Architects have also made a distinct impression.

If I have omitted to mention

19

Singapore Conference Hall and Trade Union House (1965). Also known as the NTUC Conference Hall, the building is designed by the Malayan Architects Co-Partnership (Lim Chong Keat, Chen Voon Fee and William SW Lim). The winning entry in an architectural competition, its functions are expressed in the building's overall form. It is a significant building and is one of the sources of innovation in post-independence Singapore.

others in this brief retrospect it is not that any disrespect is intended but to linger too long at this point will perhaps serve to confuse and distract from the main theme — innovation.

The years from independence to early 1980 saw practically every major architectural style from the West repeated in Singapore. Writing in 1979[29], Tay Kheng Soon identified the various 'isms' which found expression. 'Brutalism' or 'Func-

tional Expressionism' was exemplified in the Singapore Conference Hall and NTUC Building by the Malaysian Architects Partnership in 1965. The various functions of this building; the auditorium, the lift tower, the toilet accommodation were all clearly expressed in this highly influential building.

A spate of design competitions which followed the NTUC Building included Jurong Town Hall won by Architects Team 3 and the Pub-

lic Utilities Board Headquarters, won by Group 2 Architects.

Another building which showed considerable innovation in its planning—the Singapore Science Centre designed by Raymond Woo — was a result of another competition. In the context of private developments, People's Park by Design Partnership, completed in 1973, was a major contribution to the discovery of shopping as recreation in Singapore — a pattern that was to be followed by many subsequent developments.

Reviewing a decade of Singaporean architecture Tay Kheng Soon identified two main themes: first, the predominant preoccupation with technology as the generator of building form; and second the masking of regimented organisations by delightful exteriors. The latter, he speculated might 'seemingly be capricious, non-rational and for purely aesthetic preference, but may in their study reveal deep fears and future hopes.'[30]

CONSERVATION

Some of the projects included in this book reflect an increasing desire to conserve buildings and areas of historical, architectural or social value. This might be seen as a paradox by those committed to modernism and for whom 'new' is synonymous with progress. The question might be put thus; how does conservation of the heritage equate with innovation?

The pursuit of cultural continuity by maintaining the physical links

20

with the past and a deeper sense of identity is all part of the movement towards a regional view that I noted at the beginning of this essay.

It seems, therefore, entirely appropriate to include some of the best conservation work in Singapore. However, a word of caution is in order. Conservation usually begins with the protection of historic monuments, thereafter the emphasis changes to the conservation of individual buildings of merit. The third phase is when society recognises the value of whole areas of the city and the final phase is (arguably) when the emphasis changes to the conservation of a living environment, that is, the conservation of the activities and social patterns that complement the physical form.

Conservation in Singapore falls broadly between the second and third categories and whilst the 'gentrification' of conserved areas is seemingly inevitable, it is arguably not totally desirable.

The majority of conservation has been directed at the restoration and adaptive reuse of the indigenous shophouse, a model transplanted from Southern China which has shown itself capable of almost infinite internal adaptations. There is still a surprising wealth of old buildings along the Singapore River, Chinatown, Little India, Kampong Glam and the cultural core of the city that are worthy of conservation. I have, under the heading of conservation, chosen several projects which illustrate the immense possibilities of

restoration and adaptive-reuse of old buildings. Some also show how sensitively designed new buildings can harmonise with those worthy of conservation.

THE FUTURE

There is already sufficient material in this book to spark off debate about the future direction of architecture. When I reviewed *A History of Singapore Architecture* in 1986, I rejected the notion suggested by the authors that future architecture will be 'dominated by Western influence.'[31] On the contrary, I did and still believe that the countries of the Asian region stand poised to assert a regional identity in architecture which is endogenous and finds its inspiration in the cultural past and the ecology of the region.[32]

I was paraphrasing William Curtis, the noted architectural historian and champion of modern architecture, but the same ideas are evident in contemporary discourse in Singapore. Tay Kheng Soon refers to it as the creation of new mythic images[33] and another academic, writer and teacher Wong Yunn Chii, suggests that we stand on the edge of a 'paradigm shift'[34]. The new mythic image that Tay Kheng Soon proposes is of the Intelligent Tropical City, a city that loves the sun and the rain and the open way of life. The unintended 'child of modernity' conceived out of colonialism has now grown up. It seeks, in the elements, its allies in a bid for freedom to imagine a new kind of

civilisation based on its endowment, rather than being content to model its future on its foster parents.[35] These are notions which give intellectual stimulus to innovation in architecture.

ENVOI

I am optimistic that the innovative spirit in Singapore's architecture will flourish. The School of Architecture which was inaugurated in 1959 as a department of the Singapore Polytechnic became a part of

The PUB Headquarters (1977). The building is the result of a competition won by Group 2 Architects (Partners Ong Chin Bee and Tay Puay Huat). It has a strong form, with Corbusien antecedents. Indeed it has been compared to Le Corbusier's La Tourette Monastery and to Boston City Hall in the USA. The cantilevered upper floors and recessed lower floors combined with deep recessed windows are a logical solution to the tropical climate. There is further attention to design for the tropics with the provision of a generous shaded ground floor outdoor concourse.

People's Park (1970-1973). Designed by Design Partnership (Partners Koh Seow Chuan, William S W Lim, Tay Kheng Soon, Gan Eng Oon and Chee Soon Wah), this complex made a major contribution to the discovery of shopping as recreation in Singapore. It also questions the rationale of modern 'zoning' whereby the functions of a city are separated into different areas. The complex which has 15,000 square metres of rentable shops, 5,000 square metres of office space and 360 apartments reinforces the site's previous role as a magnet for people. The development, highly innovative at the time of its conception, is in the spirit of Le Corbusier's 'Unité d'Habitation'. It has lessons for the designer and can be seen as the forerunner of developments such as Balestier Point (p. 64). It retains the spirit of neighbouring Chinatown and has been acknowledged as the first shopping centre of its kind in South-east Asia.

Singapore Science Centre (1975). Raymond Woo & Associates captures the spirit of the search, in the mid-1970s, to arrive at forms which symbolised Singapore's entry into the age of high technology. The building is firmly rooted in modernism and yet its faceted facade looks for a climatically responsive architecture.

the Faculty of Architecture and Building and Estate Management of Singapore University in 1969.

As a Faculty of the National University of Singapore, its first degree course, the BA (in Architectural Studies), was granted recognition by the Royal Institute of British Architects in 1981, and its professional degree, the B.Arch achieved recognition in 1984. There have been some eminent teachers in the School's relatively short history, amongst them Donald Notley, KC Chung, Lim Cheong Keat, Lee Kip Lin and David Lim. An essential feature of the courses is the understanding of culture and climate as generators of building form.

A glance through the project teams associated with the buildings illustrated in this book gives some indication of the quality of graduates from the School of Architecture at NUS and their contribution to innovation. Names such as Mok Wei Wei, Eugene Seow, Leong Weng Chee, Patrick Chia, Kenneth Loh, Richard Ho, Low Boon Liang, Victor Loh and many others will, in years to come, no doubt become as well known as their predecessors.

In recent years, the Housing and Development Board, the Urban Redevelopment Authority and the Public Works Department have all employed some of the top graduates of the School of Architecture. This 'new blood' may be reflected in the refreshingly original ideas apparent in some recent public buildings.

The best of the young graduates emerging from the School of Architecture are deeply aware of universal values, but are equally conscious of the uniqueness of their regional culture and the dangers imposed by Western hegemony. Placing Singapore's architecture within this context presents an immensely exciting challenge for the present generation of architects.

Footnotes

1. Adami, Eddy in *Criticism in Architecture* (editor Robert Powell), No. 3 in the series 'Exploring Architecture in the Islamic World'. Aga Khan Award for Architecture. Concept Media. Singapore. 1989.

2. Ricoeur, Paul. *Universal Civilisation and National Cultures in History and Truth*. Evanston. 1965. pp.271-284 and quoted in Kenneth Frampton *Modern Architecture. A Critical History*. Thames and Hudson, 1980.

3. Adami, Eddy in *Criticism in Architecture*. Ibid.

4. *The Straits Times*. Singapore. August 30, 1988. p.13.

5. Lee, Brig-Gen Hsien Loong. *The Straits Times* Editorial. 15 July 1988 and report on 11 July 1988.

6. *The Straits Times*. Singapore. October 31, 1988.

7. Serageldin, Ismail. *Space for Freedom*. Aga Khan Award for Architecture. Butterworths Architecture. 1989.

8. Tay Kheng Soon. 'Cultural Identity in Architecture' in *Architecture and Identity* (editor Robert Powell). No. 1 in the series 'Exploring Architecture in the Islamic World'. Aga Khan Award for Architecture.

Concept Media. Singapore. 1983.

9. Lim, William SW. *A Tale of the Unexpected*. Special Commonwealth Association of Architects Session. International Union of Architects (UIA) Congress. Brighton, U.K. 13-17 July 1987.

10. Choe, Alan FC. *Objectives in Urban Renewal*, first Congress of the Singapore National Academy of Science. Singapore. 14 August 1968.

11. Lim, William SW. *A Tale of the Unexpected*. Ibid.

12. Tay Kheng Soon. *A World Class City deserves a World Class Architecture*. Conference on 'Towards Excellence in the Built Environment'. Singapore. 3-4 December 1987. p.2.

13. Tay Kheng Soon. *A World Class Architecture*. Ibid.

14. Tay Kheng Soon. *A World Class Architecture*. Ibid.

15. Liu Thai Ker, Chief Executive Officer, HDB. Foreword to *Designed for Living*. Singapore. 1985.

16. Liu Thai Ker. Ibid.

17. Lim, William SW. 'Public Housing and Community Development — the Singapore Experience' in *MIMAR: Architecture in Development*. No.7. Jan-Mar 1983. pp. 319-327.

18. Edwards and Keys. *Singapore — A Guide to Buildings, Streets, Places*. Times Books International. Singapore. 1988.

19. Tay Kheng Soon. Avant Garde Architecture in Singapore, Building Supplement. *Business Times*. Singapore. November 30th 1988.

20. Lim, William SW. *A Tale of the Unexpected*. Ibid.

21. Tay Kheng Soon. *A World Class Architecture*. Ibid.

22. Tay Kheng Soon. *A World Class Architecture*. Ibid.

23. Serageldin, Ismail. *Space for Freedom*. Ibid.

24. Serageldin, Ismail. *Space for Freedom*. Ibid.

25. Tay Kheng Soon. *A World Class Architecture*. Ibid.

26. Seow Eu Jin. *Architectural Development in Singapore*. Unpublished PhD Thesis. University of Melbourne. 1974. p. 352.

27. Yeang, Kenneth. Former President of PAM in conversation with the Author. June 1988.

28. Seow Eu Jin. Ibid. p. 356.

29. Tay Kheng Soon. *The Architecture of Rapid Development*. School of Architecture Journal. National University of Singapore. 1979. pp. 5-11.

30. Tay, Kheng Soon. *The Architecture of Rapid Development*. Ibid.

31. Beamish, Jane and Fergusson, Jane. *A History of Singapore Architecture*. Graham Brash, Singapore. 1985. p.177.

32. Powell, Robert. *Regionalism in Architecture*. Singapore Institute of Architects Journal. Nov-Dec 1986. No.139. pp.36-39.

33. Tay Kheng Soon. *Notes on the Intelligent Tropical City*. Paper read to a seminar on 'Heritage and Change in South-east Asia'. South east Asian Study Group for Architecture and Urbanism and Aga Khan Program for Islamic Architecture. Singapore. 17-28 August 1988.

34. Tay Kheng Soon. *Avant Garde Architecture in Singapore*. Ibid.

35. Wong Yunn Chii. *Precedents, Paradigms and Design*. Unpublished academic paper. National University of Singapore, School of Architecture. September 1988.

23

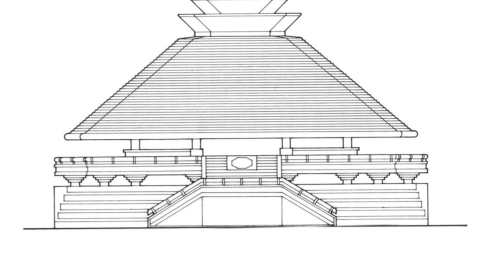

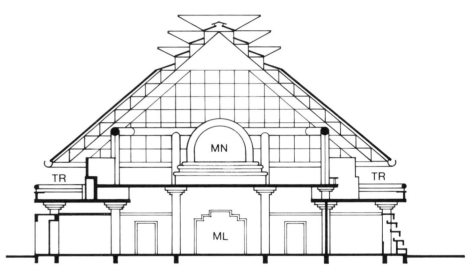

CHEE TONG TEMPLE

Elevation of the entrance facade of the temple. In deferrence to its neighbours the pyramidal roof has chamferred corners.

Section through Chee Tong Temple. The main structure of the roof is a bright red steel frame with a system of mirrors mounted on the rooftop to reflect light into the altar area.

Plan of second storey.

K Kitchen
ME Main Entrance
ML Multi-purpose Room/ Hall
MN Main Hall
OF Office
TR Terrace

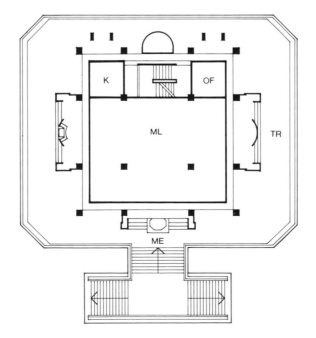

CHEE TONG TEMPLE
HOUGANG AVENUE 3, SINGAPORE 1953

ARCHITECT: AKITEK TENGGARA

COMPLETED: 1987

CLIENT
Chee Tong Temple

ARCHITECT
Akitek Tenggara

PROJECT TEAM
Tay Kheng Soon (Partner-in-charge)
Ho Kwon Cjan (Project Architect)
Patrick Chia (Project Architect)

CONSULTANTS
Structural Engineer
Houkehua Consulting Engineers
Quantity Surveyor
Akitek Tenggara
Landscape Architect
Sim Kern Teck

MAIN CONTRACTOR
Hiap Kian Hoe Construction

(Overleaf)
Chee Tong Temple in its context of the HDB
New Town of Hougang.

Akitek Tenggara is one of the architectural practices in Singapore which has consistently attempted to express a modern response to climatic conditions and the 'deep structure level of human consciousness'[1]

The Chee Tong Temple is arguably the most controversial of recent religious buildings which cater to the spiritual and community needs of the Singaporean Chinese.

When the initial designs were introduced to the public, Tay Kheng Soon described it as being "without the traditional trappings of old-time temples." However, he said that "worshippers will still recognise it as being Chinese, but the spirit is modern — it has not borrowed literally from the past".[2]

This prompted an immediate retort from Richard KF Ho who, alleged that "in not literally borrowing images from the past, the temple may have lost what could be its only link to a Chinese temple for its users".

"What is wrong" asked Ho, "if the borrowed images provide a connection for the users of the space to the particular activity that they went to the space for. Why shouldn't these images be used?"[3]

This discourse continues; there are those who share the designer's belief that the building "seems to have touched some deep common chord of consciousness and that it confirms that architecture can be made to respond to deeper imperatives than those obvious and literally stylistic motifs used as convenient signs and symbols of identity in a pastiche manner".[4]

On the other hand others argue that "the main entrance being from the side dilutes the processional quality to the altar contained in more traditional temples and detracts from its formality".[5]

Whichever side one takes in this debate, it is true to say that few buildings in Singapore can generate this level of intellectual discourse on the meaning and form of modern architecture. In what he has termed a "Transformative approach to the design of a Chinese temple," Tay Kheng Soon has described how, at the outset, Akitek Tenggara stressed to the temple trustees who commissioned the building in 1983, that they wished to interpret the design in contemporary terms. This was acceptable to the client but the whole process of design was carried out in 'consultation' with 'the master' — through a medium, who in all their consultations was in a trance. The medium, a middle-aged lady, spoke in the voice of an ancient Chinese man.

The design philosophy was discussed at various stages of its development, through the medium.

The medium agreed to the modern approach in the design and conceded that the building had to be made contemporary in response to contemporary situations. The shape of the roof and the choice of materials was agreed; the temple, it was agreed, should be light and airy, and in deference to its neighbours, the pyramidal roof of the original design should have chamferred rather than sharp corners.

Various numbers were agreed on, in consultation with the medium, specifically that the building should have three distinct level changes.

To achieve the bright and airy quality that they wished for the interior, the architects have used a system of mirrors mounted on the rooftop to reflect light into the altar area. The meaning that several observers have read into these mirrors (which were conceived as optical devices) is that they are 'a lotus'; a Chinese symbol of purity and sacredness.

Clearly the controversy about the appropriateness or otherwise of the building is part of its appeal — every worshipper or observer can bring his own meaning to the building.

At every level: spiritual, technological and in the detailed resolution, Chee Tong Temple represents an intense intellectual search for appropriate architecture for a specific time and place.

As such, it is arguably one of the finest buildings designed and built in Singapore in the last ten years.

1. Tay Kheng Soon in *MIMAR: Architecture in Development issue 27*. Concept Media, Singapore. March 1988, p.46-53.
2. Tay Kheng Soon in *Sunday Times*. Singapore. 15 April 1984. p.11.
3. Ho, Richard KF. *What Qualifies as Successful Architecture*, in Sunday Times. Singapore. April 22 1984.
4. Tay Kheng Soon. *MIMAR 27*. Ibid.
5. Cheng, Peter. Unpublished Essay. School of Architecture, National University of Singapore. 1988.

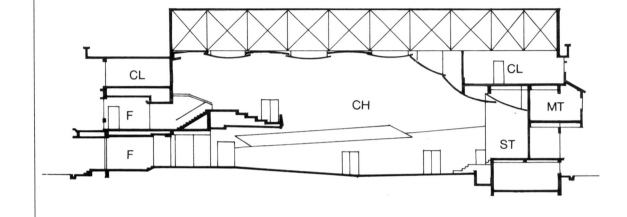

CHURCH OF OUR SAVIOUR

Section through the main hall of the church. The former cinema has been remodelled to create surfaces that resonate and to give focus to the stage.

Second storey plan indicating the additions to the former cinema. A multiplicity of forms contrast with the original box.

A Administration
CH Chapel/ Church
CL Classroom
CN Conference Room
F Foyer
MT Meeting Room
OF Office
SC Secretary
ST Stage

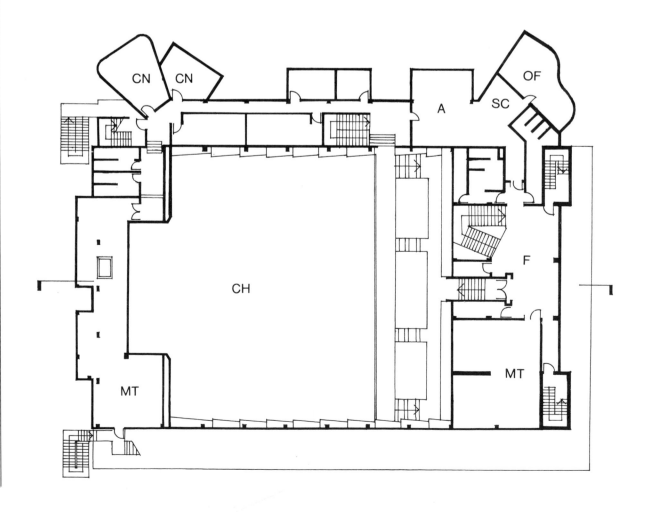

CHURCH OF OUR SAVIOUR
130 MARGARET DRIVE, SINGAPORE 0314

ARCHITECT: WILLIAM LIM ASSOCIATES

COMPLETED: 1987

CLIENT
Church of Our Saviour

ARCHITECT
William Lim Associates

PROJECT TEAM
William Lim (Partner-in-charge)
Mok Wei Wei (Partner-in-charge)
Leong Koh Loy (Project Manager)
Yip Yuen Hong
Lim Jin Geok
Daniell Wong

CONSULTANTS
Structural Engineer
Steen Consultants Pte Ltd
Mechanical and Electrical Engineer
Steen Consultants Pte Ltd
Quantity Surveyor
Simon Lim, Oh & Teo
Acoustic Consultant
CCW Acoustics Pte Ltd

MAIN CONTRACTOR
Techfield Pte Ltd

Church of Our Saviour is a provocative building which challenges our assumptions about what form a Christian Church should take. The traditional church form accommodated a liturgy which is a far cry from many present day forms of worship where chancel, nave, choir, transcept and side aisles are arguably redundant.

The architect was faced here with an intriguing brief: to convert a former cinema to its new use — a formidable problem, which the design team chose to do by 'deconstructing' the parts. This fragmentation of the elements in the plan and their individual expression whilst maintaining the harmony between the disparate parts, is reminiscent of American architect Frank Gehry's work.

However, is it an appropriate architectural language? Certainly, if we can first free our minds from preconceptions about what is appropriate for a church. This building does not alienate the public, it 'speaks' a popular language, it communicates openly.

Mok Wei Wei, the project architect would argue that the form of this church essentially grew out of the client's brief and not from any preconceived notions. The main emphasis of the charismatic churches, unlike the traditional is on 'the works and the power of the Holy Spirit' and the most striking aspect of Church of Our Saviour is its form of worship. It is a celebratory occasion which begins with singing accompanied by a band complete with piano, violin, electric guitars, cymbals, drums and xylophone. This is complemented by the congregation's spontaneous expressions. Individuals sway or dance, clap and speak of visions and prophesies. A scrmon is followed by more spirited singing, ending in rounds of applause.

The task of the architects was to translate this celebratory, guilt free spirit into tangible forms.

The essential character of the former cinema was of a rather mundane 'box', with a measure of luxury focussed on the details in the public foyer and verandah. The architects decided to capitalise on the 1960's aesthetics which used mozaic tiles in various coloured patterns and a blue and silver checkered ceiling.

Due to site constraints the additions to the building are located on the Margaret Drive elevation facing a public car park. The multiplicity of forms is intended to contrast with the existing box, but more importantly to give, in its vibrancy and dynamism, a visual celebration which complements the spirit within the church.

The interior has been strikingly remodelled to create wall surfaces that resonate and to give focus to the stage. The almost totally white interior is infused with an 'uplifting' quality, with dramatic highlighting of several celestial elements in the form of planets and clouds.

The interior has been acoustically rebalanced, though not entirely successfully, so that the congregation — speaking in tongues or singing can be heard clearly.

A stage has been created where the cinema screen used to be. Extensive remodelling has created two additional floors with rooms for meetings, Sunday School and teaching. In all, 1,000 square metres of usable space has been added.

The juxtaposition of the various elements, and the bold use of colour externally, adds to the initial discomfort of the image; yet such is the assurance of the designer that the remains of the old co-exist harmoniously with the new. What is more, there is an exuberance and audacity that blows away doubts.

If doubts do remain, it is possibly because good design has for so long been synonymous with 'modern' design. Several generations of architects were nurtured on the modernist creed that 'form followed function', whereas architects now increasingly talk about 'pluralism' and the search for a more communicative architecture. This divergence highlights the absurdity in the notion that there can be a single universal style[1].

In the finished building, we are not conscious of the old and the new, but of a fusion of past and present into a harmonious whole — perhaps that in itself is a fitting symbol for a church, and in a broader sense, reflects a society which is pluralistic and yet has a sense of harmony.

1 Tan Hock Beng. *Interior Quarterly.* March/May 1988.

The fragmentation of the individual elements of the plan, whilst maintaining the harmony between the disparate parts, is reminiscent of the work of the American architect Frank Gehry. The juxtaposition of the elements is done with exuberance, and the harmony that is achieved is a fitting symbol for the church.

The interior of the former cinema is almost totally white — infusing it with an uplifting and airy quality. Several celestial elements in the form of planets and clouds are dramatically highlighted.

The multiplicity of forms is intended to contrast with the rectangular form of the old cinema, but more importantly, they also give a vibrancy and dynamism which reflect the lively spirit of the church.

DARUL AMAN MOSQUE
CHANGI ROAD/SIMS AVENUE, SINGAPORE 1441

ARCHITECT: HOUSING AND DEVELOPMENT BOARD

COMPLETED: 1986

CLIENT
Majlis Ugama Islam Singapura

ARCHITECT
Housing and Development Board

When Islam was brought to Southeast Asia, the form of early mosques was frequently that of a tripartite pitched roof. Such mosques were common in Malaysia, Brunei and Indonesia and it was only later that the middle-eastern 'dome' became inextricably linked, for many people, with Islamic religious buildings.

Darul Aman Mosque reverts to the early pitched roof model. Although the three tier roof structure is not used in this case, there are nevertheless distinct echoes of the past in the somewhat literal interpretation of the Malay 'pondok' (hut). As with other mosques built in Singapore in recent years, this building has been designed by the Housing and Development Board for the Majlis Ugama Islam Singapura (Muslim Religious Council of Singapore).

The pitched concrete tiled roof with broad overhangs firmly roots this building in the tropics. There is a consistent use of roof forms and decoration throughout the building. This consistency sees the geometry of the steel roof truss over the main prayer hall and the forecourt repeated in small details atop the perimeter concrete wall.

The limits of the site and its access dictates that the car park which is shared with a housing block, be at the rear of the mosque. This results in the rear gate becoming as well used as the main entrance. To some extent this defeats the important function of main and rear entrances in segregating male and female worshippers, since the back entrance, originally intended to serve as a female route, is now used equally by men.

Some observers have criticised the definition of spaces in the building. There should be a hierarchy of domains from the least sacred to the most sacred in the layout of mosques, and in this respect, the forecourt is felt to be a little short. Again this can probably be attributed to site constraints.

The cool and inviting verandah space is a successful transition from the outside to the inside. Passing through the entrance foyer, there is a distinct change in the spatial hierarchy — the covered courtyard is ten to twelve metres high, full of light and breezes. Beyond the courtyard is the main prayer hall. Surprisingly, this area appears relatively darker than the covered courtyard — even though the centre is raised higher. Thus, a sense of smallness is created and one Muslim observer has noted that the hierarchy of domains required in an Islamic environment is suggested, but not fully carried through[1].

Similarly, the quality of light in the main prayer hall is not totally convincing. The 'clarity of a vision of God', which should be created by light radiating from above is not evident; only a small amount of light penetrates through the lantern light at the apex of the roof. The skylight is more significant in its external form than from inside.

The visual symbols in a mosque should be geometric, and this is appropriately done using variations of a square. These symbols are carried out in metalwork, in timber and in tile patterns on floors and walls. The fretwork beneath the gutters and the design of the doors are abstracted from Malay patterns and this is appropriate.

One unhappy compromise is the choice of light fittings which shows much less care than other details. Like the digital display announcing prayer times, these fittings jar in what in most other respects is a warm and tactile building.

The overall strategy for the plan and form of the building is successful. One can instantly recognise the most important places and the towering minaret acts as an orientation point for the surrounding area.

Darul Aman Mosque is one of the best new buildings by the Housing and Development Board — it indicates an ability to look for, and respond to, the deeper underlying structures of society. It is capable of being assessed on many levels — not simply as good building practice, but also at an intellectual level. When more buildings such as this are attempted, the standard of architectural design will transcend the utilitarian and enter the realm of art. Darul Aman Mosque makes a substantial contribution to finding an Islamic architectural language relevant to a modern city or country.

1. Rajmah bte Tahib. Unpublished Essay. School of Architecture, National University of Singapore. 1988.

33

The geometry of the steel roof truss across the main prayer hall and the forecourt is repeated in details on the perimeter wall.

The pitched tiled roof, with broad overhangs, firmly roots this building in the tropics. It is a literal interpretation of the Malay *pondok* (hut) of the region.

The visual symbols in a mosque should be geometric and here, they are variations of a square. The symbols are carried out in metalwork and timber, as well as in the tile patterns on the floors and walls.

There is a consistent use of roof forms throughout the building. The traditional *meru* form is reinterpretated with a steel truss and concrete tiles.

The towering minarct, although not fulfilling its traditional function as the vantage point from which the *muezzin* calls Muslims to prayer, is nevertheless an important symbol and also an orientation point for the surrounding area.

The skylight is more significant in its external form than from within. Inside, only a small amount of light penetrates through the apex of the roof.

34

TAMPINES NORTH COMMUNITY CENTRE

The first storey plan combines two elements; firstly, the structured perimeter frame and secondly, the casual 'free-form' activity blocks within the frame.

Section through Tampines Community Centre highlights the fragmented spaces found within the perimeter wall.

36

CC Child Care
GR Games Room
HC Homecraft
LG Lounge
OF Office
ME Main Entrance
ML Multi-purpose Room/Hall
ST Stage
SQ Squash Court
TR Terrace

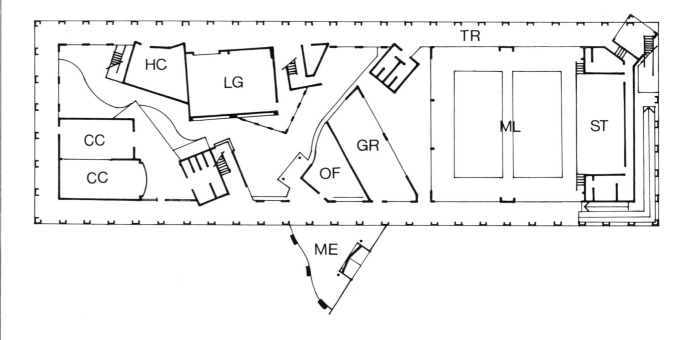

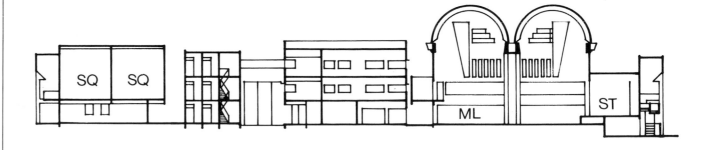

TAMPINES NORTH COMMUNITY CENTRE
TAMPINES STREET 41/AVENUE 7, SINGAPORE 1852

ARCHITECT: WILLIAM LIM ASSOCIATES

COMPLETED: 1989

CLIENT
People's Association

ARCHITECT
William Lim Associates

PROJECT TEAM
William Lim (Partner-in-charge)
Mok Wei Wei (Partner-in-charge)
Beh Ngiap Kim (Project Manager)
Ong Chee Soon

CONSULTANTS
Structural Engineer
Steen Consultants Pte Ltd
Mechanical and Electrical Engineer
Steen Consultants Pte Ltd
Quantity Surveyor
Rider, Hunt, Levitt and Bailey

MAIN CONTRACTOR
Haxxon Pte Ltd

The design of Tampines North Community Centre combines two basic elements. Mok Wei Wei, the project architect, describes these as firstly, the highly structured 'circulation frame' which defines the perimeter of the building, and secondly, the free-form, casual 'activities blocks' contained within the frame. "Together," he says "these two elements contrast yet complement each other to form a coherent statement".

Mok Wei Wei is in fact describing a metaphor of Singapore society in the late 1980s. The encompassing perimeter wall can be seen as the strongly ordered social structure. Within the perimeter wall, a variety of elements and value systems are expressed as individual fragments.

Together, this can be seen as Singapore's multi-cultured society held together by a well defined order.

The fragments of the building, like the society they mirror, sometimes burst out of the ordered constraints; more frequently they can be observed in harmonious relationships within the structured geometry of the complex.

In this, the most recent of their completed projects, the practice of William Lim Associates confirm their avant-garde status, as one of the practices attempting to articulate a truly contemporary Singaporean architecture. The practice strives to simultaneously situate itself within the international mainstream movements and to reflect regional aspirations. This 'search', as it has

been called in other contexts, is apparent in other works by the same practice such as Unit 8, Church of Our Saviour, Villa Chancery and William Lim's earlier pioneering work with Malayan Architects Co-Partnership, Design Partnership and DP Architects.

The Tampines North Community Centre building explores deeply the definition of community. It goes beyond the concept of a community centre as an anonymous, flexible, multi-use box. It strives to produce a place of distinctive character, a landmark in the town, and a point of orientation, identification and involvement for the community.[1]

The architects have endeavoured to reflect the government's drive to enhance the quality of life. The building recognises that as Singaporeans grow more affluent and sophisticated, they appreciate the finer things in life. It was the stated intention to inspire in the users of the Centre, a unique and stimulating experience both spatially and visually.

The Community Centre is prominently located at the corner of Tampines Street 41 and Avenue 7 on a roughly rectangular site. The form of the building is of a three-storey high rectangle defined by a frame of regularly-spaced twin columns — what the architects term 'The Circulation Frame'.

In this sense, the building complements the ordered facades of the surrounding HDB flats, but its scale distinguishes it from the housing. The Frame contains a main

circulation corridor linking all the activities of the Community Centre.

Within this frame, four main blocks and two smaller ones — each being expressed in a different size and shape — house specific activities. They define open spaces within the frame, creating a variety of spatial experiences.

The environment within this perimeter frame is highly complex with the various elements arranged in a three dimensional collage.

This intrinsically dual nature in the building can also be seen as a reflection of the duality in Chinese culture though the 'Chineseness' is not a conscious action by the designers. It is both formal and yet casual, ordered and dynamic, authoritarian and playful.

Leaving aside the discussion on the many levels of meaning in the building, the building responds to the tropical climate with the layering of the facade by a variety of sun shading devices and a reinterpretation of the traditional five-foot way. The major spaces are naturally ventilated and there are numerous shaded outdoor spaces.

Tampines North Community Centre is undeniably one of the best modern buildings in Singapore. It is replete with cultural references and the reinterpretation and transformation of cultural patterns. It bears comparison with the best of modern architecture in the world.

1. Hartati, Marie. Unpublished Essay. School of Architecture, National University of Singapore. 1988.

There is an intrinsic duality in the design, firstly the highly structured 'circulation frame' which defines the perimeter of the building, and secondly, the free-form, casual 'activities blocks'. These two elements contrast and yet compliment each other to form a coherent statement.

The building responds to the tropical climate with the layering of the facade by a variety of sun shading devices and a reinterpretation of the five-foot way.

It was the stated intention of the designer to inspire in the users of the centre, a unique and stimulating experience both spiritually and visually. In this, the architect succeeds, showing a confident mastery of a complex architectural language that transcends mere utility.

The building goes beyond the concept of a community centre as an anonymous, flexible, multi-use box. It is a place of distinctive character: the fragments of the building, like the society they mirror, sometimes burst out of the ordered constraints. More frequently they can be observed in harmonious relationship within the ordered geometry.

39

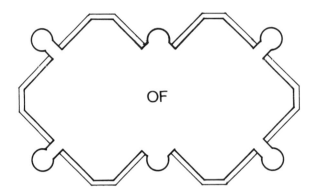

**TELECOMS RADIO RECEIVING STATION —
YIO CHU KANG**

Plan. The building is sited on the highest
level of the undulating landscape.
(For security reasons the details of the
internal layout cannot be shown.)

Elevation showing the main entrance.
Wide projections above and below the
windows give protection from sunlight
and solar heat gain.

Elevation. At basement level is a naturally
ventilated staff restaurant set in a landscaped 'amphitheatre', shaded by the first
storey of the building.

ME Main Entrance
OF Office
RS Restaurant

40

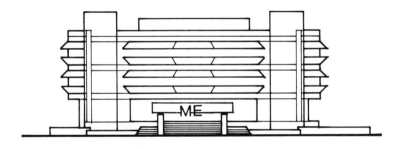

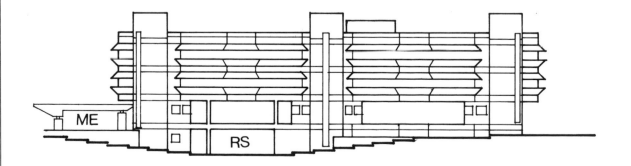

TELECOMS RADIO RECEIVING STATION — YIO CHU KANG
YIO CHU KANG ROAD, SINGAPORE 2880

ARCHITECT: ARCHITECTS VISTA

COMPLETED: 1986

CLIENT
Telecoms

ARCHITECT
Architects Vista

PARTNER-IN-CHARGE AND PROJECT ARCHITECT
Kim Loh Fong

CONSULTANTS
Structural Engineer
Leong Consultants Pte Ltd
Mechanical and Electrical Engineer
Monenco Asia Pte Ltd
Quantity Surveyor
WT Partnership

MAIN CONTRACTOR
Seah Construction Pte Ltd

(Overleaf)
The building makes a simple but powerful statement which is easily identifiable with the function. It is a thoughtful and crisply fashioned building with a precise quality of detailing.

Standing in a field of radio antennae on the elevated part of a 41 hectare site, the Telecoms Radio Receiving Station at Yio Chu Kang looks not unlike a recently landed spaceship. The image is totally fitting though its concrete 'legs' give it a permenance which prevents one from taking the analogy too far.

The architect's intention was to make a simple but powerful statement which is easily identifiable with the function of the building. In this, they have achieved a large measure of success.

The detailing of this building invites closer analysis. The architect has returned to the very basics of a good tropical building and reinterpreted the basic responses into modern technology. The functional considerations of the building skin are simple — it must create shade, cut down glare, shed the rain, insulate the interior from excessive heat gain and be durable in the tropical climate. One sees these timeless considerations ignored in so many new buildings by architects nurtured on the smooth skin aesthetic of western corporate architecture, an architecture often derived from temperate climates.

It is refreshing, therefore, to see a building which fulfils all these criteria and it is fitting that the details have already received a design award from the Singapore Institute of Architects (SIA)[1].

The detail which was specifically commended by the SIA is the protection given to the external walls. Above and below the 1.4 metre glazing slots that run around the building at second and third storey, are 4-millimetre thick Alucobond panels fixed to galvanised steel frames. The cladding panels which project 1.4 metres from the wall throw rainfall away from the building and create 100 per cent shading of the windows to an angle of 45 degrees. Furthermore the panels are heavily insulated with an air space which creates a 'heat sink'.

This ventilated space between the panels and the building structure ensures that solar heat gain is not transferred into the building.

This is an ingenious technical solution and yet remarkably simple. The detail also permits the equipment operators who spend much of their working day at computer consols to have visual relief without excessive glare.

Externally, the detail contributes to the precision appearance of the building. The Anodic Silver Flurocarbon coated Alucobond panels give a smooth horizontal surface which contrasts with the vertical circulation and service legs.

These legs appear rather heavy for a building of such modest height. The explanation is that the building is planned for future extension upwards by as much as four floors.

The quality of detailing goes beyond the external facade. The overall plan configuration is of two interlocking octagons with projecting circular circulation cores. Entering the building via a necessarily strict security process, one steps into a three storey octagonal atrium. The standard of finishes and fittings are high — almost lavish, creating a working environment where one is constantly reminded of quality and efficiency. The coordination of light fittings and return air grills is satisfactory is the manner in which the Air Handling Units (AHUs) are forced into the built form — almost a reversal of the modernist creed in this instance.

As a whole, the building is an exception to the biggest single criticism that I have of almost all the buildings that were considered for inclusion in this book — that the standard of detailing and finishes often erodes what is an otherwise fine building. Kim Loh Fong's approach to detailing is worthy of study as it is an example for future buildings in Singapore.

This project exemplifies the transformation of traditional responses to climate in modern materials. The former may hardly be recognisable in its new form, but a consistent logic is discernable.

In total, this is a thoughtful building, crisply fashioned and one which sets a very high standard for future statutory authority buildings. However, its precision is slightly marred by the rather overlarge 'Telecoms' sign, which, given the array of antennae in the vicinity, is hardly necessary. A more modest sign would have been quite adequate.

1. Singapore Institute of Architects. Micro Design Award. 1986.

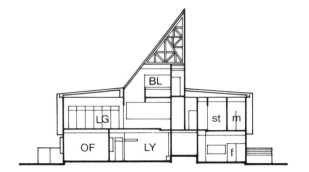

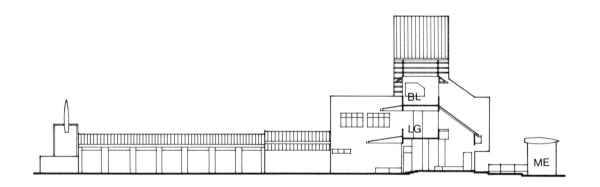

EAST COAST SEA SPORTS CENTRE

Section through the mono-pitched roof.

Section through the storage yard and the main entrance.

The plan is simple and functional.

44

BL Balcony
CL Classroom
LG Lounge
LY Lobby
ME Main Entrance
OF Office

f female
m male
st storage

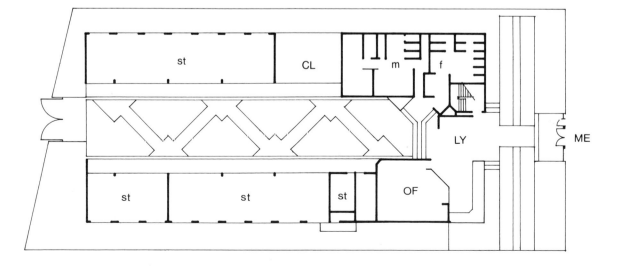

PEOPLE'S ASSOCIATION EAST COAST SEA SPORTS CENTRE
EAST COAST PARKWAY, SINGAPORE 1646

ARCHITECT: ARCHURBAN ARCHITECTS PLANNERS

COMPLETED: 1987

CLIENT
People's Association

ARCHITECT
Archurban Architects Planners

PROJECT TEAM
Mok Yew Fun (Partner-in-charge)
Tan Cheng Siong (Partner-in-charge)
Lee Mun Hoe (Project Architect)

CONSULTANTS
Consulting Engineer
Tan Ee Ping and Partners
Quantity Surveyor
KPK Quantity Surveyors

MAIN CONTRACTOR
Greatearth Construction Pte Ltd

This is a popular building which expresses the colourful, youthful sport of wind surfing. The architect has captured in the form of the building, the zest and energy of young sea sports enthusiasts in the island republic.

The plan is simple and functional, which accounts in part for its success. Built in the East Coast Park and situated conveniently on a rectangular site alongside a camping ground, the centre is less than 20 metres from the shoreline. A large gate opens onto two long open storage sheds, for storing boards, sails and rescue craft, built at right angles to the palm-fringed beach.

Facing East Coast Parkway is a reception office which has a window for supervising the 'yard' and 'classroom' areas. A flight of stairs gives access to the naturally ventilated lounge area and viewing deck at the second and third storeys.

The striking symbol of the centre is the high monopitched roof, clad in grey-blue profiled metal sheet. In the gables of this roof are two eye-catching stained glass patterns — a somewhat literal interpretation of the colourful sails which tack back and forth across the water on the seaward side of the Centre.

The form of the building immediately conveys its purpose and there is, furthermore, a consistency in the design of the perimeter fence and the entrance gates. The whole atmosphere is one of spontaneity, friendliness and enjoyment, whilst the materials used are hardwearing and effective.

The main yard is surfaced in interlocking concrete blocks, colourful, hardwearing and of a tactile texture. As designed, the project meets the demands of a society which increasingly values its leisure time, and where young Singaporeans wish to explore and use the natural world as a counterpoint to urban life.

The colourful appearance of the building at night further enhances its appeal. The graphics could have been reduced, as the very form of the building conveys its purpose, making the large sign inappropriate.

The function, materials and colours are synthesised into a coherent, light-hearted essay in a modern architectural language, with a hint of social commentary. It is synchronic with the popular literature of Philip Jeyeratnam; a building which reflects changing values of a society in rapid transition.

Fifty-four per cent of Singaporeans are under the age of 30 and were not born at the time of the struggle for independance. That struggle honed the values of the first generation of post-independance leaders which then found architectural expression in the massive public housing programme and the international style banking and commercial buildings of the 1960s and 1970s. With the reassessment of 'core values' and the discussion on national ideology comes a parallel search for a unique Singaporean architectural identity.

The non-institutional appearance of the Sea Sports Centre, its accessibility and inviting appearance convey just the right image. This is in tune with the opportunity it provides for young Singaporeans to practice sports denied them until fairly recently due to a lack of public facilities. Previous to this, the sport of wind surfing was largely the prerogative of privileged members of the few private clubs.

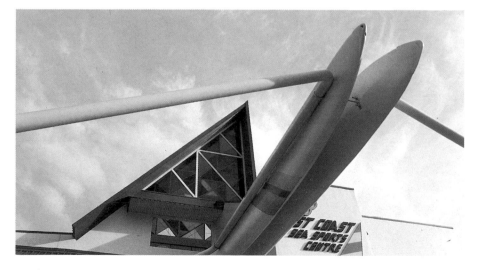

The Sea Sports Centre is less than 20 metres from the shoreline. A gate opens onto two long storage sheds for storing boards, sails and rescue craft.

Materials are robust and effective. The main yard is surfaced in interlocking concrete blocks. It is non-institutional in appearance and its image has the feeling of openness, spontaneity and friendliness.

The form of the building conveys its purpose and there is a consistency in the design. The high monopitched roof, clad in grey-blue profiled metal sheets, is a somewhat literal interpretation of a sail.

47

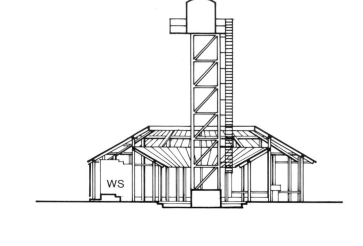

SARIMBUN SCOUTS CENTRE

Section through an ablution hut.

First storey plan. The centrepiece is the Main Assembly Hall.

Section. The main hall is 22 metres in diameter — a column free circular space topped with a square pyramidal roof.

CT Canteen
DM Dormitory
MN Main Hall
WS Washroom

48

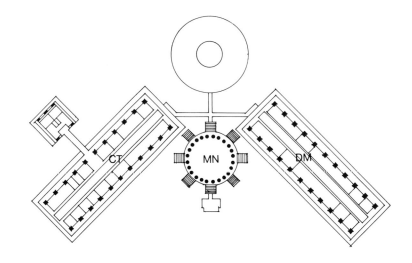

SARIMBUN SCOUTS CENTRE
JALAN BAHTERA, SINGAPORE 2471

ARCHITECT: AKITEK TENGGARA

COMPLETED: 1986

CLIENT
Boy Scouts Association of Singapore

ARCHITECT
Akitek Tenggara

PROJECT TEAM
Tay Kheng Soon (Partner-in-charge)
Eugene Seow (Project Architect)

CONSULTANTS
Engineer
Houkehua Consulting Engineers
Quantity Surveyor
Rider, Hunt, Levitt and Bailey

MAIN CONTRACTOR
KH Goh

A complete escape from city life? Back to nature? Is it possible in the rapidly urbanising island of Singapore? At the very end of a narrow road on the north west coast of the island there is just such an idyllic retreat. The place is Sarimbun Scouts Centre designed by Akitek Tenggara for the Boy Scouts Association of Singapore.

The project sets out to embody the principles of Baden Powell, the founder of the Scout movement, giving the campers the opportunity to commune with nature, to learn respect for all living things, to be taught survival techniques and to give an outdoor classroom for observation, contemplation and renewal of the inner spirit. The simple aims of the earliest Scout Camp on Browning Island in the UK are as relevant to society today as they were at the outset. Here too, in Singapore, is the need for the fellowship that grows out of a shared set of principles, of 'roughing it' in basic accommodation, of overcoming mutual fears, and finally, the comradeship of the campfire.

All these aspects were contained in Akitek Tenggara's brief, and it is to their credit that they have created a camp which, whilst giving a degree of comfort, does not remove the challenge and the fun of camping.

The centrepiece of the project is a twenty metre high Main Assembly Hall — a column free circular space, twenty-two metres in diameter topped with a square pyramidal roof. The hall sits on a ramped earth mound on an axis from the entrance gate fronted by the main field. Behind is the traditional campfire circle — emphasising its 'backwood' quality. The floor of the main hall was originally of beaten earth, the columns faced in rough hewn vertical timber boarding and the bases are protected by coils of thick rope. It is regretable that the earth floor has subsequently been tiled.

The main structure is exposed timber trusses rising to a central ring beam. The building generates a rugged, outdoor quality.

Flanking the main hall are two dormitory blocks. Here again the emphasis is on simplicity, a salubrious life and bringing the camp users close to nature. Thus, cross ventilation and simple construction technology is the order of the day.

A corrugated metal roof deck and the lack of gutters ensures that whilst tucked up in a dry bunk for the night, the young scouts will certainly experience the sound of rain and the smell of sea breezes.

The ablution blocks are similarly inventive in the use of basic and tough technology which one observer has likened to that of the 'pioneer' corrugated metal aesthetic of Australian architect Glenn Murkutt[1].

Elsewhere on the extensive site which overlooks the Straits of Johore and the south coast of Malaysia, the original trees have been retained, with a number of challenging character-building tests involving ropes and pulleys rigged to some of the larger specimens.

For the more experienced campers, there are cleared areas of relatively flat ground for tents. Nature is used naturally at Sarimbun and not simply for decoration.

The success of Sarimbun Scout Centre is in how it has captured the spirit of scouting, both in the relationship of the buildings to the terrain and in the limited, but wholly appropriate, choice of materials. The low-energy, resource-conserving form of the buildings, and the natural ambience of the whole site, makes one wish that in the master planning of the island of Singapore, more such sites, far away from the air-conditioned bedroom, the 24-hour convenience store and the NTUC taxi fleet, could be made available. Ultimately, one appreciates all the luxuries of life more for being temporarily deprived of them.

I have one criticism of the camp arising from a weekend spent there in the company of some handicapped young people. In common with many buildings in Singapore, not sufficient consideration is given to the use of the facilities by people in wheel chairs or on crutches, but the remedy is simple — a few earth ramps constructed by the Scouts themselves would quickly solve the problem.

This project is in sharp contrast to the Serangoon Gardens Country Club and the Chee Tong Temple, other projects by the same practice. It demonstrates the flexibility and inventiveness of Akitek Tenggara.

49

1. Wong Mun Summ. In conversation with the Author. October 1988.

The centrepiece of the Scout Camp is a twenty-metre high Assembly Hall. The hall, fronted by the main field, sits on a ramped earth mound on an axis from the entrance gate. It relates well to the terrain.

Flanking the main hall are two lower blocks. The emphasis is on simplicity and bringing the users close to nature. Thus, cross ventilation and simple construction technology is the order of the day.

The ablution blocks are inventive in the use of basic technology. In some ways, it resembles the corrugated metal aesthetic of Australian architect Glenn Murkutt.

The floor of the main hall was originally of beaten earth, regretably it has subsequently been tiled. Elsewhere, in the timber boarding and the coils of thick rope, the details capture the essence of scouting.

50

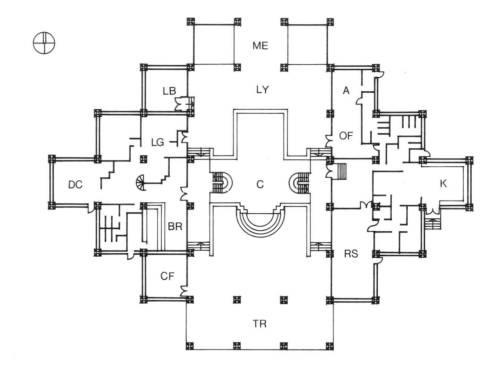

SERANGOON GARDENS COUNTRY CLUB

First storey plan. The plan is generated from a square module which is expressed in the structure.

Section. The main activity rooms of the club are related to the central space with a finely choreographed play of levels.

Section. At the heart of the club is a glass covered room of exhilarating proportions.

A Administration
BR Bar
C Court
CF Cafe
DC Discotheque
F Foyer
52 **FN** Function Room
K Kitchen
LB Library
LG Lounge
LY Lobby
ME Main Entrance
MT Meeting Room
OF Office
RS Restaurant
TR Terrace

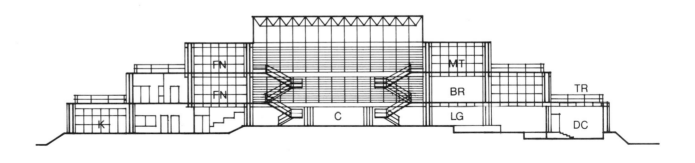

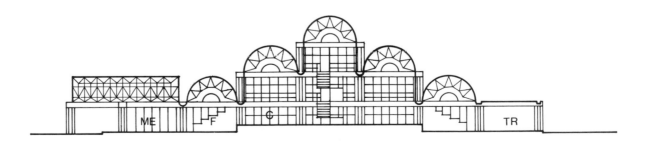

SERANGOON GARDENS COUNTRY CLUB

KENSINGTON PARK ROAD, SINGAPORE 1955

ARCHITECT: AKITEK TENGGARA

COMPLETED: 1986

CLIENT
Serangoon Gardens Country Club

ARCHITECT
Akitek Tenggara

PROJECT TEAM
Tay Kheng Soon
(Partner-in-charge)
Eugene Seow (Project Architect)

CONSULTANTS
Structural Engineer
Structural Executive Decision
Inc Pte Ltd
Mechanical and Electrical Engineer
Loh and Aw Consultants
Quantity Surveyor
Langdon Every and Seah
Landscape Architect
Belt Collins and Associates

MAIN CONTRACTOR
Greatearth Construction Pte Ltd

At the heart of the Serangoon Gardens Country Club is a huge glass-covered garden room of exhilarating proportions. Here, all the activities of the club members are focussed in a naturally ventilated space; a space where one can sit and sip a refreshing drink whilst waiting for a friend, lounge under a tropical moon in the evening and even occasionally enjoy a performance by a string quartet.

Central to the success of the project is a total reappraisal of what makes living in the tropics different, what makes it unique. Thereafter, the architects have endeavoured to capture all the positive aspects without the discomfort of excessive glare, heat, or humidity.

This has involved not only careful planning of the facilities, but also the integration of highly sophisticated cooling and shading devices in the glass vaulted roof.

The plan of the main clubhouse is generated from a square module, and is expressed externally in the form of five glazed barrel vaults — the centre vault being the highest, the two adjoining vaults a storey lower and the outer two vaults the lowest.

The main activity rooms of the club are related to the central landscaped space. A carefully orchestrated interplay of levels and staircases gives access to the restaurant, library, lounge bar, discotheque and cafeteria. In contrast to the naturally ventilated garden, these facilities are air-conditioned.

Generous planting in the central area and careful choice of furniture gives an image of relaxed sophistication. Trees, paving and planting containers are organised to define space and focus direction, screening out undesirable views.

The sporting activities of the Country Club are separate from the main clubhouse at the opposite end of the Olympic size swimming pool. Members can select from four squash courts, a gymnasium, aerobic activities or sauna bath.

The form and elevation of the sports annex, although subdued in deference to the main building, is totally in keeping with the main clubhouse structure.

The success of this project is in the consistency of design from the initial idea, to the detailing of fenestration, services and landscape. The modular square grid is expressed in the structure, the exposed concrete waffle slabs and the aluminium window grills. Each structural column is made up of four smaller elements. The space between the small columns accommodates variously, lighting or access panels to concealed services. Particularly innovative is the incorporation of nylon sun screens in the roof structure. These screens can be activated electronically as and when weather conditions demand.

In the end bays of the glass barrel vaults are extract fans, and along the sides are fixed glass louvres designed to expel warm air. Although this arrangement is not totally successful in achieving comfort conditions at all times, it is infinitely preferable to the ubiquitous air-conditioned lobby.

Akitek Tenggara have earned a reputation for their consistent search for a relevant architecture both for the tropics and for Singapore. The majority of their buildings question both at an intellectual level and a practical level what is suitable for the tropical climate and, by inference, what is appropriate to the Singaporean life-style.

The facilities in a fairly exclusive country club may not be accessible to the vast majority of Singaporeans, but the ideas explored, and for the most part successfully implemented, can be reproduced in other buildings for public and private use. The nature of innovation is that it explores new frontiers in technology and finds new expressions of traditional cultural patterns.

The key issue in contemporary architecture are "modernism versus traditionalism, internationalism versus regionalism and technology versus craft"[1]. Tay Kheng Soon's architecture is at the very heart of this discourse — he attempts to articulate a tropical, modern regional architecture which harnesses technology to create new and viable forms without recourse to the neo-vernacular. This approach is at almost the opposite end of the spectrum to the forms adopted, for the Singapore Polo Club (p. 56) or the Swiss Club extensions (p. 60).

53

1. Serageldin, Ismail. *Space for Freedom.* Aga Khan Award for Architecture. Butterworths Architecture. 1989.

Here is an attempt to articulate a modern regional architecture, harnessing technology to create new and viable forms without recourse to the neo-vernacular.

To respond to the tropical sunlight, screens are incorporated in the roof structure. These nylon screens are activated electronically when weather conditions demand. In the end bays of the glass barrel vaults are extract fans and along the sides, fixed glass louvres.

A carefully orchestrated interplay of different levels and staircases adds to the drama of the glass-covered garden room.

The nature of innovation in this project is that the architect explores new frontiers in technology and new expressions of traditional cultural patterns to create a striking built form for the tropics.

55

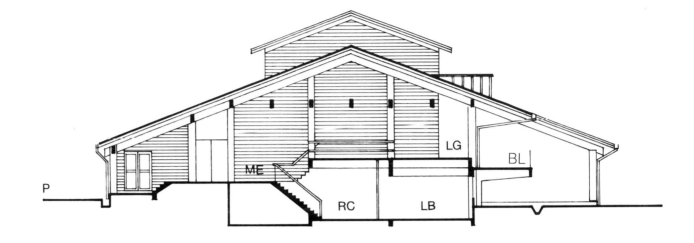

POLO CLUB

Section. The external verandahs are protected by wide overhangs which give adequate cover from rain and sun.

The club house has an open plan; the bar, lounge and restuarant are all oriented towards the polo field.

BL Balcony
D Dining
K Kitchen
LB Library
LG Lounge
M Machine Room
ME Main Enterance
P Parking
RC Reception
SQ Squash Court
SW Swimming Pool

f female
m male

56

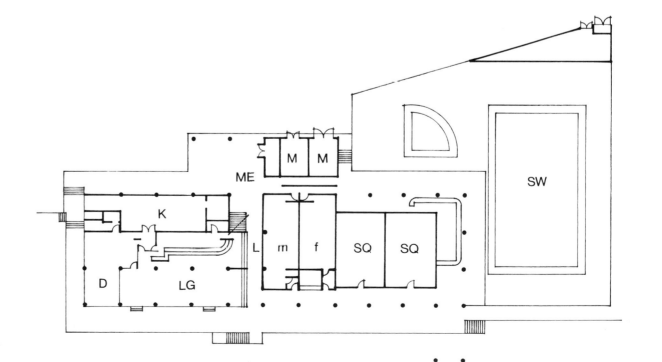

SINGAPORE POLO CLUB
THOMSON ROAD, SINGAPORE 1129

ARCHITECT: IAN LANDER ARCHITECT

COMPLETED: 1985

CLIENT
Singapore Polo Club

ARCHITECT
Ian Lander Architect

PARTNER-IN-CHARGE AND PROJECT ARCHITECT
Ian Lander

CONSULTANTS
Structural Engineer
RJ Crocker Russell
Mechanical and Electrical Engineer
CT Partners
Quantity Surveyor
WT Partnership

MAIN CONTRACTOR
Seng Giap Construction Pte Ltd

Innovation can take many forms, but the underlying premise is that a building must contribute to the search for an architecture which is appropriate to a time and a place — in other words to a regionally appropriate architecture. In a sense, this will generate a hybrid architecture —drawing from the past, vernacular buildings, but firmly rooted in the modern society of Singapore.

For certain types of buildings, the traditional form is highly suitable, and thus, when presented with a brief for premises for the Singapore Polo Club, Ian Lander sought for a precedent in the colonial houses of the past, which themselves drew both on European renaissance models and on the traditional Malay kampong house.

This is a literal interpretation of the traditional dwelling comparable with the approach of Gordon Benton in the Swiss Club extension. The result is an impressive clubhouse which also serves as a spectator stand when games are in progress.

The clubhouse has an open plan with the principal rooms, the bar, lounge and restaurant, all orientated towards the polo field—a broad tree fringed arena. The game itself is associated with the colonial era, though the 'Game of Kings', as it is known, originated 2500 years ago in Iran and was a popular royal pastime in China for many centuries. It was passed on to India, Asia Minor and Japan, but as the Eastern empires declined, the game fell into obscurity until rediscovered by the British. The Singapore Polo Club was established in Balestier Road in 1895, moving to its present location in 1937. The game still attracts a number of expatriates, but there are a larger number of local players, and matches are regularly played against teams from Brunei, Malaysia and further afield.

The architect has used fair faced red brickwork, richly stained and polished timber and brass fittings extensively in this building. Using traditional craftsmanship, the quality of detail is meticulous in the bar fitting, screens and balustrades. The external verandahs are protected by wide overhangs which give adequate cover from rain and sun while the pitched roofs contain a number of solar panels for heating water. 'Chick' blinds (bamboo or wooden slatted blinds) can be lowered to prevent the ingress of rain during thunderstorms.

The Polo Club uses traditional forms and crafts in a completely timeless manner. It achieves what a good 'tropical' building should possess; one passes effortlessly from inside to outside, from secure to non-secure areas, from private to public areas without uncomfortable barriers. An atmosphere of relaxed sophistication is achieved.

Perhaps more importantly, it dispels the notion that modern buildings in the tropics have to be air-conditioned to be comfortable. By appropriate design, orientation, high internal volumes, cross ventilation and shaded verandahs, the traditional forms produce architecture which is not only comfortable but also energy efficient. This must be a serious consideration as energy costs rise and fossil fuels, we are informed, are rapidly being depleted.

There are, after all, many valuable lessons to be learned from tradition.

The architect draws heavily on traditional architectural language and forms for the clubhouse. The neo-vernacular design uses high internal volumes, cross ventilation and shaded verandahs to produce comfortable conditions which are energy efficient.

The building achieves what successful tropical architecture should; one passes effortlessly from inside to outside, from the secure to non-secure areas, and from private to public sections without uncomfortable and obvious barriers.

There is an atmosphere of relaxed sophistication in the Club bar which overlooks the playing field. The architect sought his precedence from both the colonial 'black and white' houses of Singapore and the traditional Malay kampong dwelling.

The architect uses fair faced brickwork, dark brown clay floor tiles, richly stained and polished timber and brass fittings. The quality of workmanship is meticulous in the bar fittings and screens.

The external verandah is protected by a wide overhang which gives adequate protection from rain and sun. Bamboo or slatted wooden blinds can be lowered to prevent the ingress of rain during storms.

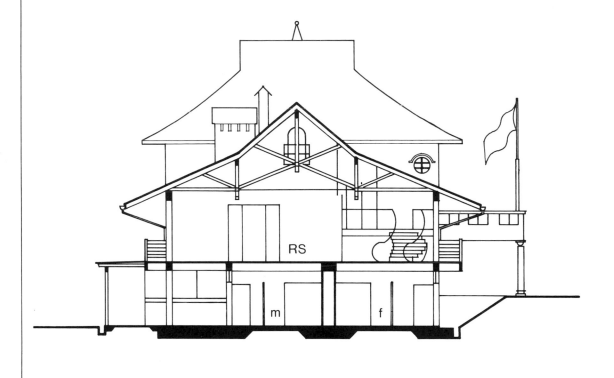

THE SWISS CLUB

Section. The restaurant has a high double-pitched roof and is naturally ventilated.

Second storey plan. The restaurant projects into the tembusu grove with a four-metre overhang at the open end.

BR Bar
F Foyer
K Kitchen
LG Lounge
RS Restaurant

f female
m male
st storage

60

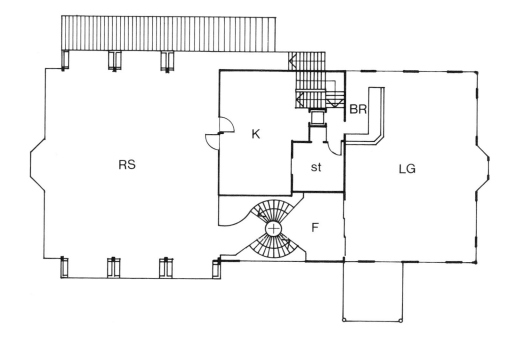

THE SWISS CLUB
SWISS CLUB ROAD, SINGAPORE 1128

ARCHITECT: GORDON BENTON AND ASSOCIATES

COMPLETED: 1986

CLIENT
The Swiss Club

ARCHITECT
Gordon Benton and Associates

PROJECT TEAM
Gordon Benton (Partner-in-Charge)
James Wong (Project Architect)

CONSULTANTS
Structural Engineer
Harris and Sutherland Pte Ltd
Mechanical and Electrical Engineer
J Roger Preston and Partners Pte Ltd
Quantity Surveyor
Partnership International McDonald
Partners Pte Ltd
Landscape Architect
BCP Far East

MAIN CONTRACTOR
Mei Hwa Construction Works Pte Ltd

Born in Kuala Lumpur, Gordon Benton has spent most of his working life in South-east Asia. He brings to his architecture, a deep understanding of, and sensitivity towards, the tropical eco-system.

The Swiss Club, part restoration and part new-build, is a fine example of how architecture can respond to, and even enhance, the natural landform and tropical forest.

The old clubhouse, built in 1927 by architect HR Arbenz, was well-described as a small 'chateau-in-the-forest'. When, in 1983, the Swiss Club committee decided to hold a limited competition for the further development of the club, many members accepted that the old building would have to be demolished to facilitate a new design.

Benton convinced them otherwise, and in his winning design report argued that the architectural quality was of such a high standard that every effort should be made to preserve the historic building.

His conviction has proved well founded and the completed project is a dialogue between old and new, the latter respecting the fine proportions and delicate fabric of the original building.

The club's requirements were for a variety of recreational facilities: four floodlit tennis courts, two squash courts, four badminton courts, a swimming pool, a multi-purpose hall with a small stage, a restaurant, lounge, changing rooms, kitchens, committee meeting rooms, offices and staff rest room.

Only the last three named areas were to be air-conditioned, all other spaces would be naturally ventilated and it was to be a test of the architect's skill to provide a cool and pleasant environment.

The *tour-de-force* of the project is the new restaurant extension with its magnificent relationship to the landscape. One dines practically in the tembusu (a tropical hardwood) grove with mature trees almost within reach. The floor is of merbau timber, with a roof over described by the architect as "a series of open triple king-post trusses restrained by three lateral girder trusses, all in timber, giving a four-metre overhang at the open end". It is a curious marriage of the double-pitched roofs of the Malay Peninsula and the dark timbered roofs of a north-European banqueting hall, but the result is totally convincing.

The roof is lit by indirect lighting, and antique fans stir the air, adding to the breezes which rustle the leaves of the nearby trees. The whole ambience is that of openness with traditional split-cane 'chick' blinds being lowered if there are storms or additional shade is needed.

The restoration of the old clubhouse has been no less sensitively carried out, the former lounge of the Swiss Shooting Club being restored and equipped with a snooker table.

The original colour scheme of the old building (red timber and white walls) has been retained, and the details of the existing windows, column heads and shutters have been lovingly and patiently restored.

Various uncomplimentary earlier extensions were removed to reveal the original elevations.

The same sensitivity is evident in the placing of the tennis courts and swimming pool. So many new buildings in Singapore start by reducing the site to a series of cleared level platforms — it takes a great deal more skill to work with the existing natural landforms and to retain mature forest specimens. Even the huge multi-purpose hall which can cater for 300 to 400 people is effectively 'lost' in the forest as are the squash courts which are set into the hillside, thus allowing the eye to travel over the roof to the trees beyond.

The whole project is a fine example of building 'with', rather than 'on', the land. It requires a knowledge of forest trees and their root and canopy structure. It is a tribute to the design team that they have retained so much of nature, and that the new buildings sit so comfortably in their surroundings.

For the extension, the designers have drawn their inspiration from the traditional built-forms of South-east Asia, the stilted kampong house set beneath shady trees and the colonial 'black and white' house which raised the principle rooms to second storey level to take advantage of the cooling breeze.

The result is a building of immense creativity and meticulous detailing. In its sensitivity to the environment and the site, The Swiss Club rivals the work of the Sri Lankan architect Geoffrey Bawa.

The *tour-de-force* of the project is the new restaurant extension with its magnificent relationship to the landscape. The architect draws inspiration from the traditional built forms of South-east Asia and brings to the planning a deep understanding of, and sensitivity towards, the tropical rain forest and its eco-system.

The old clubhouse, built in 1927 by architect HR Arbanz, was fittingly described as a 'chateau-in-the-forest'. The restoration of the original building has been sensitively carried out — various uncomplimentary extensions were removed to reveal the original elevations.

62

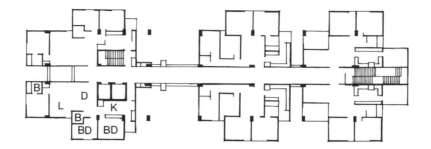

BALESTIER POINT

Plan of ninth storey. The units are grouped symmetrically along a corridor.

Section. The lowest two floors and the sub-basement are a shopping complex. Car parks occupy the third and fouth storeys while apartments are from the fifth to the eighteenth storey.

64

B Bathroom
BD Bedroom
D Dining
G Garage
K Kitchen
L Living
SH Shop
SM Shopping Mall

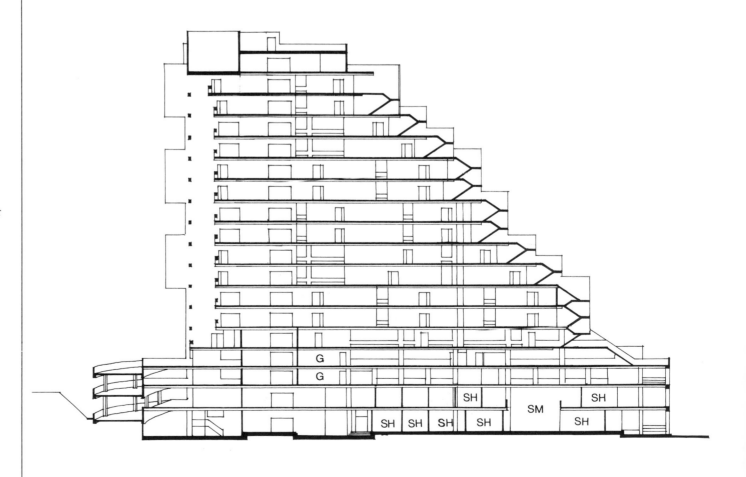

BALESTIER POINT
BALESTIER ROAD, SINGAPORE 1232

ARCHITECT: REGIONAL DEVELOPMENT CONSORTIUM ARCHITECTS

COMPLETED: 1986

CLIENT
Central Plaza Development Pte Ltd

ARCHITECT
Regional Development Consortium
Architects

PROJECT TEAM
Chan Fook Pong (Partner-in-charge)
Huang Siong Hui (Project Architect)
Leong Weng Chee (Project Architect)

CONSULTANTS
Civil and Structural Engineer
Tan Ee Ping and Partners
Mechanical and Electrical Engineer
Design and Management Services Pte Ltd
Quantity Surveyor
Building Cost and Management
Consultants

MAIN CONTRACTOR
Takenaka Komuten Co. Ltd.

The influence of Moshe Safdie, with whom Regional Development Consortium collaborated on the Habitat project in Singapore's Ardmore Park, is evident.

The form of the 18-storey mixed commercial and residential complex is derived by stacking a series of cubes in pairs, rising from the fifth storey to two penthouse units. The lowest two floors and the sub-basement are a shopping complex with a variety of neighbourhood facilities such as hairdressers, beauticians, florists and a McDonalds outlet. Car parks occupy the third and fourth storeys.

The mix of commercial tenants appears to be successful and there is a lively atmosphere.

The upper floors of the project give the impression of being precast concrete boxes, though, in fact, it is an *insitu* concrete frame with rendered brick infill.

The juxtapositioning of the various modules and their subsequent painting in white and various shades of pink is confidently handled by the designer. The modelling of the blocks furthermore creates a harmonious inter-play of solid and void, of light and shadow.

This geometric precision is at once enhanced and softened by roof terraces planted with shrubs and flowers, and by green pergolas supported by restraining rods. The entrance to the shopping complex has had careful attention given to landscaping, including fountains and a small pool in the forecourt.

The scale of the building is reduced by the complex and highly articulated relationship between the residential units and the considerable variation in the fenestration. The owner of each unit must have some feeling of individuality compared with many dwellers of modern slab blocks buildings. Thus, the architecture is seen to incorporate attitudes which K. Nagashima suggested as early as 1970[1] would develop in Singapore — a need for diversity rather than homogeneity, identity rather than anonymity, choice rather than conformity; a gradual transformation in social principles.

The scale of the complex is further reduced by what the architects term 'an abstraction of the five-foot way, which in the past provided a sense of intimacy in tropical buildings, in the form of a framed hollow cube'. This frame is evident on the first two storeys and sub-basement of the podium block fronting Balestier Road. However one regrets that more life could not have been instilled by spilling some of the shop activities onto the corridor such as one finds in traditional shophouses.

The individual residential units are grouped symmetrically along a central corridor, but any notion that this will result in a dark and forbidding space is immediately dispelled. The 'sky-bridges' are light and breezy with distant views of the urban landscape. The corridor is well protected by cantilevered units on both sides though some

observers feel that the space is slightly inhospitable because of the lack of articulation of entrances and the absence of windows in the walls. Nothwithstanding this and the slight problem of glare due to the contrast of lighting levels along the corridor, it is still pleasant to walk along and is a good climatic solution in the tropics.

The residential units have ten variations of plans through the different orientation of roof terraces, though the external form imposes some constraints on the internal circulation.

The project is a further development of a type which was introduced into Singapore with the People's Park Complex in 1973.

The building is not without its faults — services are not as well integrated into the design as in the Habitat building. This is not uncommon in many new Singapore buildings and may be the result of responsibility for location and design of services falling somewhere 'between' the roles of the various professionals. Here, it results in a rather unsightly arrangement of water and sewerage pipes on the exposed soffits.

In general however, the building is well mannered and gently exerts its presence. It is a vigorous addition to Balestier Road and transforms urban architecture into poetry.

65

1. Nagashima, K. *Leisure and Social Change.* Seminar on Planning for Recreation. Singapore Planning and Urban Research Group, 1970.

The juxtaposition of the apartment modules and their subsequent painting in white and various shades of pink are confidently handled. A framed hollow cube structure, an abstraction of the traditional five-foot way, reduces the scale of the complex and signals the main entrance.

There is a geometric precision in the complex and a highly articulated relationship among the residential units. Variation is introduced in the positioning of fenestration to introduce individuality in each of the residential apartments.

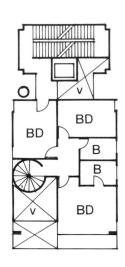

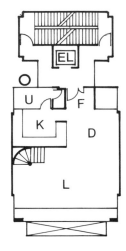

NO. 11 INSTITUTION HILL

Plans of a two-storey apartment with the living room at the lower level. The main rooms and balcony spaces overlook the heavily wooded Institution Hill.

Section of the eleven storey building.

B Bathroom
BD Bedroom
D Dining
EL Elevator/ Lift
F Foyer
K Kitchen
L Living
U Utility
v void

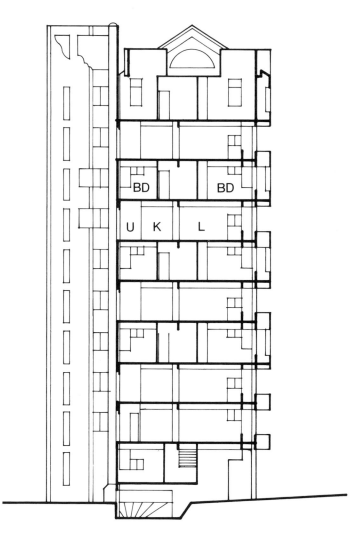

NO. 11 INSTITUTION HILL
SINGAPORE 0923

ARCHITECT: TANGGUANBEE ARCHITECTS

COMPLETED: 1988

CLIENT
Cosy Housing Developments (Pte) Ltd

ARCHITECT
TangGuanBee Architects

**PARTNER-IN-CHARGE AND
PROJECT ARCHITECT**
Tang Guan Bee

CONSULTING ENGINEER
Houkehua Consulting Engineers

MAIN CONTRACTOR
Cosy Housing Developments (Pte) Ltd

Is there a place for humour and playfulness in residential architecture? If, as it has been said, Singaporeans are moving into the 'self actualisation' phase described in Abraham Maslow's stages of human development[1], then there is presumably a place for creativity and initiative, more variagated forms, humour and freedom of expression.

Perhaps this 11-storey residential block of 5 maisonettes located on a hilly site just off River Valley Road is a forerunner of the kind of colour and playfulness that we can expect if this creativity is unlocked.

The project responds to the client's request for 'a building with character', on a tight site of 600 square metres and a limited budget. The main rooms and balcony spaces turn away from the main road toward Institution Hill, a heavily wooded plot of land upon which sit several grand old colonial mansions, unfortunately now in a state of advanced decay.

The building immediately attracts the attention of people travelling along River Valley Road towards the city. It towers above the surrounding low-rise houses and announces its presence with a brash and colourful plummage.

The number 11 is a cut-out in the concrete staircase core and bright purple, yellow, orange, pink and green enliven the concrete structure.

The elevations show the hand of a confident artist. The juxtaposition of light and dark, solid and void, and the interplay of geometric forms, highlighted by splashes of colours, are no less than a work of art, a vast three-dimensional modern sculpture with each elevation capable of being an independent graphic composition.

This is quite an appropriate choice for residents who wish to tell the world, "Here I am!", rather than live behind an anonymous and homogeneous form. This can be seen as a probable direction towards the end of this century as Singaporeans demand and avail themselves of choices.

The corollary to this is that No. 11 Institution Hill is itself a finite form and will not easily lend itself easily to modification — the same architect's work on the Mandalay Terrace Housing shows a difficulty that can arise where more open forms are not used, and in consequence, the harmony of the composition can be disturbed when individual owners embellish their own apartments.

The individual apartments of No. 11 Institution Hill are conventionally planned. A typical unit is two storeys high with open plan living-dining space on the lower level which, together with the kitchen, are accessed from the lift lobby. The upper floor has three bedrooms, one of which can be independently accessed from the stair and lift lobby.

A circular staircase in a double volume space gives internal access between the two floors.

The workmanship, as in so many buildings in Singapore, is quite disappointing; principally the inability to co-ordinate and plan service pipes. The basement entrance is for this reason a letdown — anticipation built up from afar is dissipated somewhat by rather crude pipework, balustrades and decoration.

This is perhaps something beyond the control of the architect — craftsmanship in terms of a well aligned pipe and a well executed joint is not valued highly and there is often an emphasis on speed and economy rather than quality and pride. Paradoxically, there are many examples in this book of diligent craftsmanship and quality finishes.

This apart, the building is marvellously inventive and quite enigmatic. It gives much visual delight, yet, its extrovert facade masks a private domain.

The thought occurs to me: if Tang Guan Bee can achieve so much variation within a tight budget, then such results are also possible in mass housing.

In analysing the semantic properties of the built form, I have constructed a number of meanings. It raises the question: what meanings are perceived by others — the residents and passers-by? It suggests an interesting field of enquiry into the communicative properties of regional modern architecture.

69

1. Tay Kheng Soon. *Architecture Journal.* School of Architecture. National University of Singapore. 1987.

If, as it has been said, Singaporeans are moving into a phase of 'self actualisation', then there is a place for creativity and initiative, and more variagated residential forms embodying humour and playfulness.

This building is inventive and quite enigmatic. It gives visual delight and yet its bold facade masks a private domain.

No. 11 towers above the surrounding low-rise houses and announces its presence with a brash and colourful plumage. The number '11' is a cut-out in the staircase core while bright coloured paintwork enlivens the concrete structure.

71

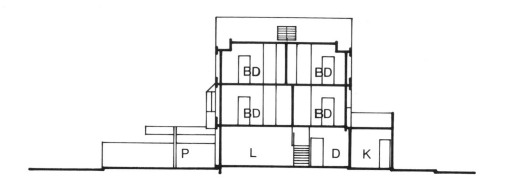

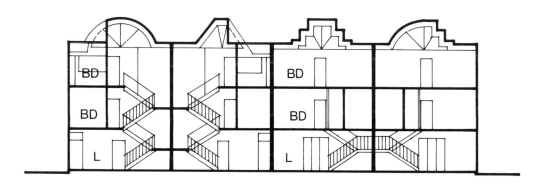

MANDALAY TERRACE HOUSING

Section through the four bedrooms.

Section.

First storey plan. Minor variations in plot depth permit two of the houses to be slightly larger than their neighbours.

BD Bedroom
D Dining
GR Games Room
K Kitchen
L Living
P Parking
TR Terrace
U Utility

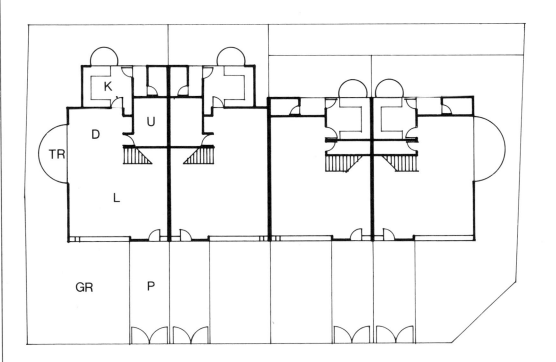

MANDALAY TERRACE HOUSING
MARTABAN ROAD, SINGAPORE 1232

ARCHITECT: TANGGUANBEE ARCHITECTS

COMPLETED: 1986

CLIENT
Joo Chek Cheong Developments
(Pte) Ltd

ARCHITECT
TangGuanBee Architects

**PARTNER-IN-CHARGE AND
PROJECT ARCHITECT**
Tang Guan Bee

CONSULTANT ENGINEER
Leong Consultants Pte Ltd

MAIN CONTRACTOR
Joo Chek Cheong Developments (Pte) Ltd

The cultural reference for this short row of terrace houses is mixed Peranakan terraces and conventional low-rise housing. The four houses were consciously conceived in the image, colours and individuality of its Peranakan neighbours.

The architect has sought to give character and identity to each house by expressing each roof differently. They are distinctive, eyecatching and immense fun whilst never descending to 'kitsch', as the proportions and articulation of the elevations are handled confidently.

For reasons of commercial viability, the architect was constrained to make each of the plans almost identical, but minor variations to the elevations and pastel colours serve to make each an individual home.

The site is relatively small and used to its maximum. Minor variations in plot depth permit two of the houses to be slightly larger than their neighbours. These have four bedrooms, each with ensuite bathroom as compared with two generous sized bedrooms in the two smaller plans.

The fenestration at second and third storey appears playful but is a rational response to the internal plan arrangements.

It is interesting to see what the owners have done with the four houses since completion. One of the terrace houses has been maintained in its original form, while another (the corner unit) has had a beautifully detailed and sensitive extension to create a covered terrace and walkway. This is in keeping with the original spirit of the house and enhances it with its appropriate choice of materials and proportions.

The remaining two houses have been drastically altered. The extensions would probably be justified in terms of giving more shade and additional rain protection, but unfortunately, they substantially alter the original design intentions of the architect.

The extensions happily, do not detract from the innovative spirit of the four terrace houses. It is a spirit that still shines through — the spirit of Singapore eclectic or 'Chinese Baroque' terraces such as one might see in Syed Alwi Road or in Joo Chiat reinterpreted into modern architecture.

The houses combine humour together with a spirited expression of individuality. They are rather frowned upon by some of their more 'conservative' neighbours, but are an expression of the spontaneity and quest for identity which Tay Kheng Soon has identified as values of a society in transition.[1]

1. Tay Kheng Soon. *A World Class City Deserves a World Class Architecture*. The Architecture Journal. National University of Singapore, 1987.

The spirit of Singapore eclectic or 'Chinese Baroque' terraces is reinterpretated in this short row of terrace houses. They were consciously conceived in the image, colours and individuality of the row houses of Syed Alwi Road and Joo Chiat.

The fenestration at second- and third-storeys appears playful, but it is a rational response to the internal plan arrangement.

The corner terrace house has been maintained in its original form, and a beautifully detailed and sensitive extension has been added to create a covered terrace and walkway.

The houses combine humour and a spirited expression of individuality. Although frowned upon by some of their 'conservative' neighbours, they are an expression of spontaneity and identity.

The architect gives character to each house by expressing each roof differently. They are distinctive and eye catching.

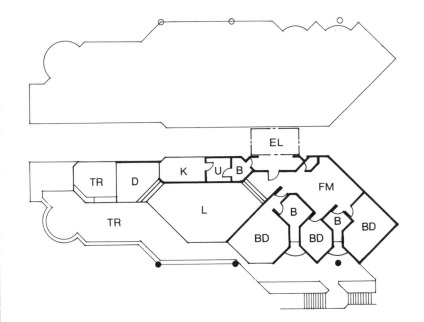

THE PALISADES

Plan of a typical apartment designed with the majority of walls at 45 degrees to the central axis thus ensuring privacy and orientating windows towards sea views.

Elevation. The architect reduces the impact of the building by extensive planting on the private roof gardens.

76

B Bathroom
BD Bedroom
D Dining
EL Elevator/ Lift
FM Family Room
K Kitchen
L Living
TR Terrace
U Utility

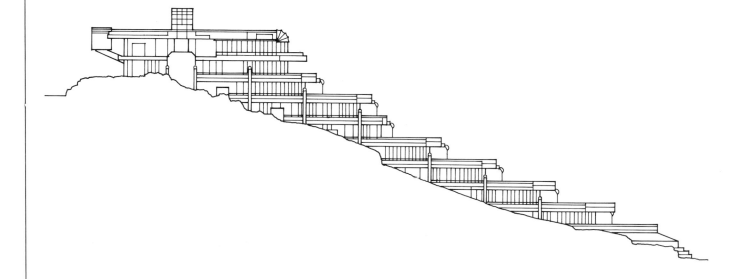

THE PALISADES
PASIR PANJANG ROAD, SINGAPORE 0511

ARCHITECT: INTERNATIONAL PROJECT CONSULTANTS

COMPLETED: 1985

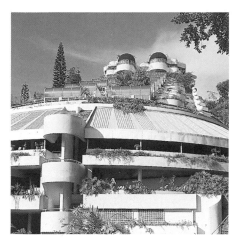

CLIENT
Palisades Development Pte Ltd

ARCHITECT
International Project Consultants

PROJECT TEAM
Geoffrey Malone (Partner-in-charge and Project Architect)
Philip Conn (Partner-in-charge)
Celina Pok
David Chew

LANDSCAPE ARCHITECT
BCP (Far East) Pte Ltd

MAIN CONTRACTOR
Palisades Development Pte Ltd

The architect's response to a narrow site on a hillside facing the Straits of Singapore is to cascade 18 townhouses down the slope, giving each a private terrace utilising the roof of the apartment below. The townhouses are arranged in pairs, serviced by a lift travelling at a 22° angle rather than vertically.

The project is a development by a consortium of individuals who came together to build the apartments for their own use.

The architect's intention from the outset was to reduce the apparent mass of the building. This they achieved by hugging the building to the hillside and applying prolific planting to the exposed structure. Viewed from Pasir Panjang Road the development evokes images of cultivated terraces found throughout Asia. The angular and curvilinear projections of the terrace structures also helps to break down the scale. Some measure of the success can be gauged when comparing the development to the adjoining, traditional tower block.

At the very summit of the hill is a barbecue area and free-form swimming pool shared by all the residents. Privacy has been assured by the retention of dense existing foliage and extensive new planting.

The apartments are designed with the majority of walls at 45° to the central axis, thus ensuring privacy with windows orientated towards the sea view. Each unit has a split-level living and dining area, a galley kitchen and attached utility area. The main bedroom has fine views and the attached bathroom opens onto a small private courtyard screened from the garden. Two other bedrooms, with a shared bathroom, open onto a family space.

The architect's own unit gives a taste of the house of the future — his creativity is given full range in the design of space age furniture, advanced lighting techniques and electronic gadgetry.

It is like stepping into a time capsule, an experience exaggerated by the relatively slow journey by 'inclinator' up the slope as if to an air-lock at the entrance of each unit. Outside the living module, the roof garden provides the inhabitants with a link with the universe and distant views of the city's life-support infrastructure.

The development is exclusive, and every effort has been made to ensure privacy for each occupant. The individual private roof gardens effectively make the units terrace houses which are arranged in a totally innovative way.

The exposed roof area has attracted some criticism on the grounds that, in the tropics, it is more sensible to protect by large overhangs rather than expose flat surfaces to solar heat gain.

Closer examination shows that the architect has in fact provided quite generous shading by cantilevering floor slabs, and has introduced passive energy conservation methods such as planted trellises and pergolas. There is provision for solar collectors to be incorporated into the configuration of the building for the purpose of heating water.

Some occupants express the view that the configuration of the apartments inhibits the natural ventilation of units, resulting in heavy reliance on air-conditioning for comfort. This is possibly true, though the external terrace gardens, particularly when cool breezes blow in from the sea in the late evening, are exquisite. Another difficulty suggested is the hazard which the inclinator shaft and the numerous steps pose to young children, though this is perhaps less real than imagined.

Utilising the steeply sloping south facing hill, it is a unique house form in Singapore. It is not uncommon to see similar arrangements on Meditteranean hillsides, but the relative lack of such topography makes it unlikely that it will be widely replicated in Singapore.

The overwhelming impression is of an inventive architect who has produced a life-style which challenges present perceptions. Not inappropriately the architect's wife is a Planner in the Ministry of National Development.

Some Singaporean observers have commented that the building can be perceived as a dragon, symbolising good luck and success. It is possibly unintentional, but it is ironic that an expatriate Australian has managed to unconsciously incorporate such a cultural reference into a building.

The mass of the building is reduced by hugging the building to the hillside and applying prolific planting to the exposed structure. The angular and curvilinear projections break down the scale.

Viewed from Pasir Panjang Road, the condominium evokes memories of the cultivated terraces found throughout Asia. The eighteen town houses cascade down the slope; each has a private terrace utilising the roof of the apartment below.

The townhouses are arranged in pairs. They are served by an elevator travelling at an angle of 22 degrees up the slope to the entrance of each unit.

The architect's own apartment is futuristic with an array of advanced lighting techniques and electronic gadgetry. The 'time-warp' experience is exaggerated by the relatively slow journey by the inclinator to the 'air-lock' at the entrance.

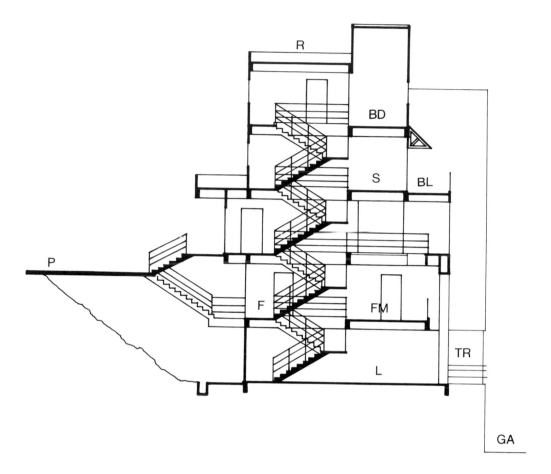

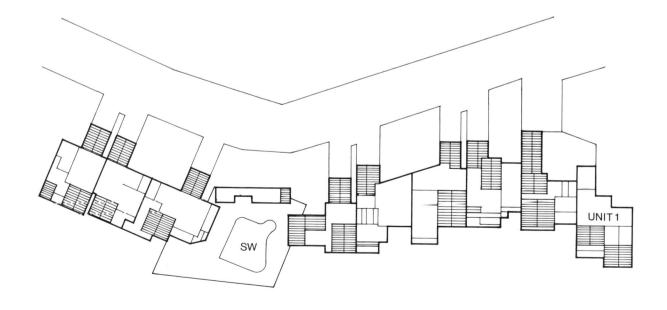

PASIR PANJANG HILL TOWNHOUSES

Section through Unit 1. The five storey row houses ingeniously exploit the slope of the hill. The entrance is from a cul-de-sac which is at approximately the height of the third storey.

Site plan. The houses are located on a hill facing Kent Ridge, commanding a view of the wooded slopes of South Buona Vista.

BD Bedroom
BL Balcony
F   Foyer
FM Family Room
G   Garden
L   Living
P   Parking
R   Roof
S   Study
SW Swimming Pool
TR Terrace

80

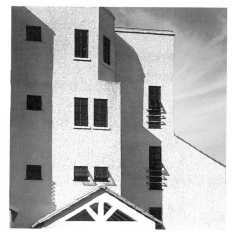

PASIR PANJANG HILL TOWNHOUSES
PASIR PANJANG HILL, SINGAPORE 0511

ARCHITECT: DP ARCHITECTS

COMPLETED: 1986

CLIENT
Tunas Jaya Lumber Pte Ltd

ARCHITECT
DP Architects Pte Ltd

PROJECT TEAM
Chan Sui Him (Partner-in-charge)
Koh Seow Chuan (Partner-in-charge)
Low Boon Liang (Project Architect)

CONSULTANTS
Engineer
Sim Bee Teck and Associates
Quantity Surveyor
Ian Chng Cost Consultants Pte Ltd
Landscape Architect
DP Architects Pte Ltd

MAIN CONTRACTOR
Neo Corporation Pte Ltd

The name of DP Architects has in recent years become associated with multi-million dollar projects including Marina Square (in conjunction with John Portman and Associates) and the Wisma Atria development on Orchard Road.

In this comparatively small project, DP Architects demonstrate that they have lost none of their ability to conceptualise innovative ideas. The nine townhouses are located on Pasir Panjang Hill facing Kent Ridge and command a breathtaking view of the wooded slopes of South Buona Vista.

While the five-storey houses (inclusive of basement) have a consistency in their architectural expression, there is significant diversity in their individual designs as reflected in the facades. Each unit is in fact custom designed to the specific requirements of its owner, and there are therefore, wide divergences in the internal layout and organisation of space.

Chan Sui Him and Koh Seow Chuan, two of the directors of DP Architects, occupy units within the terrace development.

The ubiquitous 'row' house is a form long associated with urban Singapore architecture, indeed the early merchants' houses were often in 'terraces' sharing common party walls. Many of the earlier terraces in Emerald Hill, Tanjong Pagar and Mount Sophia are now enjoying a new lease of life.

This townhouse development is a realistic alternative to the large condominium, and has many possible applications on small urban sites. In this case, a number of close acquaintances formed a company for the purpose of building the houses for their own use. It is a method which several other consortiums are turning to.

The planning of the individual units ingeniously exploits the slope of Pasir Panjang Hill. The houses are entered from the quiet cul-de-sac which is at approximately the height of the third storey. This has enabled the architects to create houses with dual entrances where two or three generations of a family might live in separate apartments while maintaining close links. Here the cultural patterns of Singaporeans are consciously woven into the building plan and section.

On the north side of the houses, a series of terraces follow the contours of the hill creating a hierarchy of spaces. The lower terraces allow access along the shared garden to a small swimming pool whilst not invading the privacy of the individual 'verandahs'. The terraces evoke memories of the terraced rice fields seen all over Asia, and are an indication of the sensitive approach to the landscape throughout the development.

The Pasir Panjang Townhouses explore a reinterpretation of the row house concept. The involvement of all the owners from the outset has resulted in the variegation of the built form, and this, together with the consistent and yet varied expression of balconies, doors and windows, introduces the notion that here is a development where all can live in harmony and each can express individuality.

It is a curious phenomena that from the early part of this century, in the urban situation, only the very poor and the reasonably rich have generally been able to build houses which reflect their own personality. In developing countries specifically, 'mass' housing has evolved, the mass being all those who are not poor enough or wealthy enough to express themselves in their housing. The notion probably goes back to the early philanthropists such as Cadbury, Lever and Titus Salt who built 'model' villages for their workforces in Britain and to methods applied to tackle the rehousing problems of post-war Europe. It is also a product of the principles of the Modern Movement which saw, in the industrialisation of housing, a means of achieving social equity and justice. Today even the condominium owner has a limited say in the design of his home.

Here, Chan Sui Him and Koh Seow Chuan have exploited a method of design and building which returns to the pre-industrial age when each owner had influence over the design of his dwelling.

It leads me to speculate firstly, whether this approach has wider application as a method of building on small or fragmented sites in the metropolis, and secondly, if the early involvement of prospective buyers or owners would be one way of personalising public housing.

81

The Pasir Panjang Townhouses explore a reinterpretation of the row house concept. The involvement of all the owners from the outset of the project has resulted in the variegation of the built form.

On the north side of the house, a series of terraces follow the contours of the hill, evoking memories of stepped rice fields.

On the private side of the row of town-houses is a swimming pool. There is, throughout, a sensitive approach to landscaping, and the lie of the units exploits the slope of Pasir Panjang Hill.

The five-storey houses have a consistency in their architectural expression, but there is significant diversity in their internal layout. This is reflected in the facades.

83

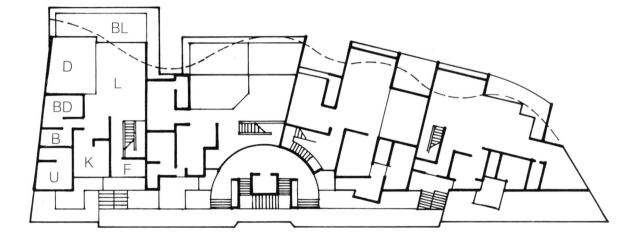

UNIT 8

Plan

Elevation to Holland Road. The flat facade has relatively small openings. The entrance is emphasised by a semi-circular pediment which interupts the roof line.

B Bathroom
BD Bedroom
BL Balcony
D Dining
F Foyer
K Kitchen
L Living
U Utility

84

UNIT 8
71 HOLLAND ROAD, SINGAPORE 1025

ARCHITECT: WILLIAM LIM ASSOCIATES
(in continuation of DP Architects)

COMPLETED: 1983

CLIENT
Unit 8 Pte Ltd

ARCHITECT
William Lim Associates
(in continuation of DP Architects)

PROJECT TEAM
William SW Lim (Partner-in-charge)
Richard KF Ho (Project Architect)
Leong Koh Loy (Project Manager)
Carl G Larson
Low Chwee Lye

CONSULTANTS
Structural Engineer
Steen Consultants Pte Ltd
Mechanical and Electrical Engineer
Steen Consultants Pte Ltd
Quantity Surveyor
Partnership International
Acoustic Engineer
CCW Acoustics Pte Ltd
Landscape Architect
Garden and Landscape Centre

MAIN CONTRACTOR
Sin Heng Construction Co Pte Ltd

Unit 8 is an intriguing building which evokes extreme reactions; you love it or you hate it. Part of this controversy is to do with its colour — synonymous with Unit 8 is the description 'The Pink Building'. The colour was chosen by Richard K F Ho, the project architect. Some others agree with the choice, saying that the colour brings out the sensuality and soft edge of the building while white gives emphasis to the 'hard edged' elements.[1]

The building is designed to respond to the site and its constraints. Holland Road is a busy highway. The flat facade that faces the road has relatively small window openings to control noise. The semi-circular 'pediment' which interrupts the straight roof line, emphasises the entrance, the tilted area of white tiles is a response to the narrowing of the triangular site. The 'rear' elevation has subtle curves and is completely different from the public frontage. It has large windows and balconies which face onto large detached houses with mature trees and well kept lawns. This could be seen as a perfectly pragmatic response — 'form follows function' to use the modernist's doctrine — but it is more than that. There is a duality introduced which has deeper roots in Chinese culture — though the architect emphasises there is no conscious effort to introduce ethnic based architectural signals.

Polarity — the contradiction of opposites is a basic principle of oriental philosophical ideas. Thus, we see in the building a duality between the flat facade of the 'outside' face and the fluid curves of the 'inside' face.

The boundary wall and the position of the gateway on the front elevation could be explained as a functional response to security and a noise barrier to Holland Road traffic. On a different level, it can also be seen as a sub-conscious interpretation of the division between the public realm and the private realm that is typical of traditional walled houses in some parts of China.

The gateway, slightly offset from the main entrance to the apartments, draws its inspiration from gateways in Chinese architecture as a threshold of movement, framing views, giving visual connection between spaces and reflecting Lao Tsu's notion of transitional relationships.

Other cultural references can be found in the steps to the 'front door' of the first storey apartments. Their *serambi* can quite plausibly be seen to have cultural roots in the traditional hierarchy of spaces in the traditional Malay kampong dwellings where there is a graduated hierarchy of privacy.

The front facade of the building has a solid and controlled appearance. It is appropriately scaled for its location on Holland Road and is punctuated with elements which externally express the internal organisation. The facade reflects internal shifts in the geometry, spatial volumes and subdivision of the units. The vertical subdivision of the facade which is within a controlling horizontal frame can be seen as an echo of the street facades of the old shophouses in Singapore.

The orientation of the building is related to the configuration of the site. In the detailed design of windows and balconies, there is a response to climatic constraints. Windows on the north of the building have deep reveals, whilst those on the south side have substantial balconies.

This duality in the building, its complex architectural image and unique identity sets it apart from its contemporaries as an exemplary piece of regional modern architecture. It is a significant and striking landmark.

William Lim, since his early days with Malayan Architects Co-Partnership and DP Architects, has been in the forefront of conceptual ideas on architecture and is no stranger to controversy. Whether one admires Unit 8 or not, the building certainly provokes discussion about the appropriateness of its 'language', and the inherent contradictions and complex meanings in the architectural expression.

1. Leong Howe Ngai. Unpublished Essay. School of Architecture, National University of Singapore. 1988.

Polarity — the contradiction of opposites is a basic principle of oriental philosophical ideas. This duality is expressed in the flat facade of the 'outside' face and the sensual, fluid curves of the 'inside' face.

The flat facade that faces Holland Road has relatively small window openings to control noise. The semi-circular 'pediment' which interrupts the straight roof line emphasises the main entrance.

The boundary wall and the gateway can be seen as a subconscious interpretation of the division between the public realm and the private realm that is typical of traditional walled town houses in parts of China. The gateway is a threshold of movement, framing views, visual connections between spaces and reflecting Lao Tsu's notion of transitional relationships.

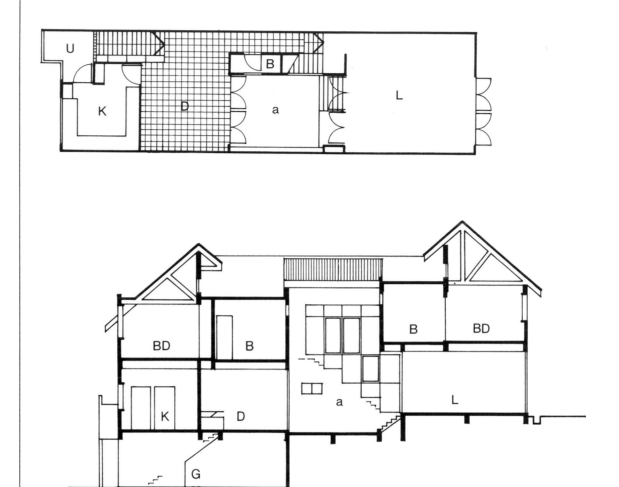

VILLA CHANCERY

First storey plan. This is a reinterpretation of the traditional Singapore terrace house.

Section. The air well which is a feature of the Singapore shophouse becomes the most prominent feature.

Villa Chancery site layout.

B Bathroom
BD Bedroom
D Dining
G Garage
K Kitchen
L Living
U Utility
SW Swimming Pool

a airwell

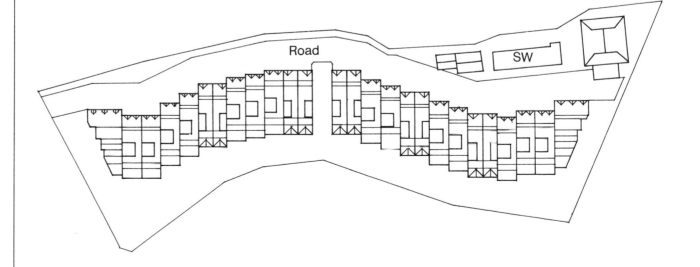

VILLA CHANCERY CONDOMINIUM
39 CHANCERY LANE, SINGAPORE 1130

ARCHITECT: WILLIAM LIM ASSOCIATES

COMPLETED: 1986

CLIENT
Villa Chancery Development Pte Ltd

ARCHITECT
William Lim Associates

PROJECT TEAM
William SW Lim (Partner-in-charge)
Carl G Larson (Partner-in-charge)
Beh Ngiap Kim (Project Manager)
Tan Teck Kiam
Leong Koh Loy
Kenneth Loh

CONSULTANTS
Project Manager
Select Management Pte Ltd
Structural Engineer
Steen Consultants Pte Ltd
Mechanical and Electrical Engineer
Rankine and Hill Pte Ltd
Quantity Surveyor
Partnership International
Landscape Architect
Garden and Landscape Centre

MAIN CONTRACTOR
Sin Heng Construction Co. Pte Ltd

As Singaporeans become increasingly affluent and better educated, there is, quite naturally, a desire to exercise their freedom of choice; choice of government, lifestyle, schools and last but not least, housing.

This is reflected in a demand for a wider variety of residential accommodation. Villa Chancery Condominium, a three-storey row house development in a subdued palette of colours, is one response to this perceived need.

The architect has introduced variety into the overall plan by breaking the row houses into groups. These are stepped back and forth in response to the site contours and the existing road to achieve privacy for individual units and an aesthetically pleasing form. The roofs of the houses are pitched in different directions.

The back of the development is to Chancery Lane. Access is via a private entrance with a semi-private road paved in interlocking concrete blocks to ensure that traffic proceeds carefully. Individual car parking is provided beneath each house.

The choice of russet red, pine green and cream-beige paint to the basic finish of all the houses results in a restrained and quietly sophisticated appearance. This is complemented by the careful detailing of lighting poles, house numbers, road verges and the landscaped areas.

The architecture of these townhouses is an attempt to reinterpretate the old Singapore terrace house. In this respect, William Lim Associates has acquired a thorough knowledge of this typology in the adaptive reuse of 98 and 102 Emerald Hill and 2 Saunders Road, the second of which is also illustrated in this book.

In this new development the airwell which is almost mandatory in the Singapore terrace house style, becomes the most prominent feature. The split-level living and dining areas open into a courtyard beneath the airwell, while the bedrooms on the upper floor relate to this space in much the same way that they do in a traditional terrace. The airwell serves another practical purpose in giving natural light to the stairwell.

The pitched roof is used to full advantage with exposed timber trusses and high volumes.

What contributes to the overall feeling of restrained good taste is the attention given to a shading detail introduced around most windows. This sort of micro detailing is not usual in Singapore, even in quite costly projects — often architects delegate such tasks to a junior draughtsman but here we see an instance where the architect's devotion is handsomely rewarded. It raises what otherwise might have been a simple functional solution to one which deserves the name — architecture. Two other details, the distinctive balcony (shaped like a house gable) and the dormer windows, give the houses their individual character.

Overall, the appearance of the project is unashamedly modern; stripped of decorative embellishment and yet of comfortable human scale and thoroughly domestic. The owner of an individual house can feel a degree of privacy while there is a sense of a small community in the shared pool and barbecue area.

Perhaps more attention could have been given to providing storage areas. Without this provision, bicycles, surfboards, shoe racks and other paraphernalia of family life are inevitably thrown into the rear of the open car ports. It would be unfortunate if individual owners decided to put doors on the garages to create concealed storage space as the rhythm of the cross walls and the open garage is another factor which gives a human scale to the whole development.

The vast majority of Singaporeans will never be able to afford a three-storey house with garden space, but there are a number of lessons in Villa Chancery. Sensitive detailing, variegations in the massing of blocks, subdued colours and the hierarchy of semi-public to private spaces show how a very simple form can be raised to the level of excellence.

Taking a traditional terrace house typology which originated from South China, the architect has cleverly reinterpreted this into modern architecture. The resulting hybrid could readily be transplanted into numerous urban situations.

Variety is introduced into the overall plan. The terrace houses are stepped back and forth in response to the site contours and the existing road line. The roofs of the houses are pitched in different directions to add individual character.

The airwell is the most prominent internal feature of the house. It is a clever reinterpretation of shophouse typology.

Attention is given to the detailing of shading devices around windows which raises the simple form to the level of excellence. The variegation in the massing of blocks, subdued colours and the hierarchy of semi-public to private spaces is equally well executed.

The choice of russet red, pine green and cream-beige paint as the basic finish of all the houses results in a restrained and quietly sophisticated appearance. This is complimented by sensitive landscaping.

APPLE COMPUTER (SINGAPORE)

First storey plan. The architects have
created an environment that inculcates
pride of the staff in the Apple products.

Section. Entering the building from the
east through a portico one enters a triple
storey atrium with a view of the production area behind the reception counter.

92 **CT** Canteen
LC Lecture Hall
LY Lobby
M Machine Room
ME Main Entrance
OF Office
PD Production Area

f female
m male

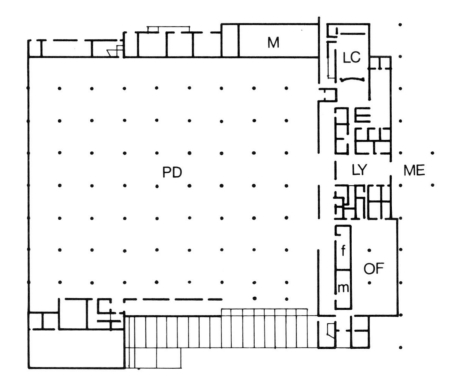

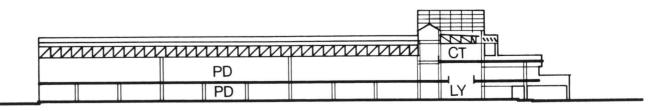

APPLE COMPUTER (SINGAPORE)
ANG MO KIO STREET 64, SINGAPORE 2056

ARCHITECT: ARCHITECTS TEAM 3

COMPLETED: 1987

CLIENT
Apple Computer (Singapore)

ARCHITECT
Architects Team 3

PROJECT TEAM
Terry Tay (Partner-in-charge)
Chris Vickery (Project Architect)

CONSULTANTS
Structural Engineer
Steen Consultants Pte Ltd
Mechanical and Electrical Engineer
Bescon Consultants
Interior Design
HED Architects
Quantoty Surveyor
Lau, Teo and Yong
Landscape Design
Garden and Landcape Centre

MAIN CONTRACTOR
Takenaka Komuten Co.

The future economic prosperity of Singapore will be founded on its ability to make and market high quality products. Its very survival depends on its ability to stay in the forefront of technology as well as remaining a stable political and economic base to attract multinational investment. The quality of Singapore's work-force is of equal importance as is the committment to producing 'high intergity' goods.

Few buildings express this better than the Apple Computer Factory and Offices in Ang Mo Kio. One's first impression of the building is that its image is absolutely fitting to its product. Sharply defined, it stands out from its neighbours for the precision of its finishes and the fact that, like a well designed computer, its peripherals are all neatly incorporated in the package.

This same precision is carried into the interior where the airconditioning ductwork and lighting fittings are exposed below the soffit, each precisely located and meticulously finished. The lighting, is not just effective in technical terms but it is used in an innovative manner to create dramatic contrast in circulation areas and an even quality of illumination in working areas. The whole ambience of the building, both internally and externally, is of clarity and precision.

Entering the building from the east through a striking transparent portico, one encounters a dramatic triple-storey atrium. Behind the receptionist are direct views of the production area. This again seems

to be a deliberate management policy, and the designers have gone to great lengths to provide visual continuity between office staff and production staff. Architects Team 3 have introduced an unobtrusive system of electrically operated fire shutters which automatically separate office and manufacturing functions in the event of a fire. Such attention to detail and an innovative approach to technical problems are evident throughout.

If one word were to sum up this building, it is surely 'quality'. Quality in the detailing of smoked glass screens to conference areas; quality in the design of perforated metal sun screens above the canteen windows; quality in the choice of Herman Miller office furniture; quality in the precision detailing of white aluminium cladding panels; and quality in the attention to the external landscape.

Here, the Apple building breaks new ground. There is no perimeter security fence around the plant, no forbidding security guard post; simply a well designed landscaping scheme which in a subtle way, says 'Private. Keep Out'.

Within the factory, the idea of quality is carried through to the non-working environment. The canteen seats 250 staff and there is a roof garden on the third floor of the office facility. In close proximity is a squash court, aerobics studio and fully equipped gymnasium — underscoring a familiar expression used by Apple's management: "Our people are the company". This

dictum is also carried into the total design of the project, as the building promotes interaction and communication at all levels.

The main circulation spine between offices and production area is highlighted by a glazed skylight at right angles to the main entry axis. This sense of drama is further enhanced by the two views at the reception counter. To the right, a narrow, compressive corridor space leads to a brilliantly lit red wall and a congenial lounge area outside the training room. To the left, an equally striking flight of stairs, flanked by dramatic uplighters, ascends to the second storey office lobby and the executive boardroom.

As one might expect in a building making a technologically advanced product, more than usual attention is given to the mechanical and electrical services. The factory boasts the first 100 per cent digital PABX system in Singapore and the company's main frame, electronic mail and outside on-line services can be assessed through the system. In the field of energy conservation, the main air-conditioning system is controlled by a microprocessor-based chiller capacity and sequencing controller.

This high technology approach and a management philosophy which places emphasis on the working environment has led to an innovative response from the architect. The result is a new standard for industrial buildings in Singapore and a new concept of quality in the working environment.

The quality of detailing in the Apple Computer building is evident in the precision of the aluminium cladding panels and in the perforated metal sun screens above the canteen windows.

The lighting is not just effective in technical terms, but it is used in an innovative manner to create dramatic contrast in circulation areas and even quality of illumination in working areas.

A sense of drama in the interior is enhanced by the two views at the reception counter. To the left, a striking flight of stairs flanked by dramatic uplighters ascends to the executive boardroom, while a compressive corridor space leads to a brilliantly lit red wall on the right.

The Apple Computer building sets a new standard for industrial buildings in Singapore and a new concept of quality in the working environment. The future and continued economic prosperity of Singapore as a Newly Industrialised Country will be based on its ability to research, make and market high quality products.

Few buildings express a committment to quality and production of 'high integrity' products as well as the Apple Computer factory and offices. Sharply defined, it stands out for the precision of its finishes and the fact that, like a well designed computer, its peripherals are neatly incorporated into the complete package.

BUKIT BATOK NEIGHBOURHOOD 3 CENTRE
SINGAPORE 2365

ARCHITECT: HOUSING AND DEVELOPMENT BOARD

COMPLETED: 1987

ARCHITECT
Housing and Development Board

The Housing and Development Board's achievements are justifiably the focus of much national pride and international attention. The Board, since its inception, has not considered itself to be in the business of producing beautiful architecture *per se*. Its role has been to implement a massive urban renewal and rehousing programme emphasising affordability, efficient delivery systems and rapid construction techniques. The result, in architectural terms, is unquestionably repetitive, and to even the most partial observer, slightly monotonous.

Against this backcloth is the Board's architects' increasing innovation in conceptualising and planning the forms employed in landmark buildings.

The 'precinct' is now the basic planning unit of every new town. Each precinct is a group of buildings intended to create a social space which is pedestrian orientated. The space contains, as a rule, a number of shops and a playground. At the next level of planning is the Neighbourhood Centre which contains numerous shops and a market, and at the highest spatial level, there is the Town Centre.

Bukit Batok Neighbourhood 3 is one of the most recent Neighbourhood Centres and its quality design augers well for the future.

The Centre has a distinct identity and a real sense of place, attributes lacking in some of the earlier HDB work. The architects have succeeded in creating a delightful stage set for the enactment of life's daily drama.

The Neighbourhood Centre has a wonderful human scale. The reinterpretation of the traditional five-foot way and the relaxed way in which officialdom turns a 'blind-eye' to its appropriation by shopkeepers as additional display area for their goods, makes it a highly successful space.

The architects have succeeded in recreating linear movement and thus increasing the possibility of meeting neighbourhood friends as in the traditional shopping streets of Chinatown or Serangoon Road. It has an urban quality that eluded many earlier designs.

At the very heart of this Neighbourhood Centre is a pedestrian square, often frequented by elderly people and small children who play in complete safety. To experience the Centre in use is to be reminded of the 'timeless patterns' in Christopher Alexander's book *A Pattern of Language*[1]. The interlocking social patterns and the richness that result makes this probably the best Neighbourhood Centre designed to date by the HDB.

There are some criticisms that can be made on the project. The adjoining Area Office responds well to the pedestrian square but is less successful on its more visible outer elevation where a lack of articulation loses the pleasant scale achieved internally. Even if it were meant to be slightly more monumental on this facade, it could still have achieved this with a more tactile and 'accessible' architecture.

Perhaps the criticism is premature, for additional buildings and public spaces are being planned for the adjoining site. This question on the 'meaning' of the facade can only be properly addressed when it is set in its final context.

The importance of this Centre will be increased, and its range of opportunities widened, when the adjoining Bukit Gombak Mass Rapid Transit station is operational. This may also give opportunities for the Centre to be linked with neighbouring housing.

A contributory factor which makes the Neighbourhood Centre so successful is the attention given to its detailing. The fretwork along the five-foot way are a clever reinterpretation of the Chinese bracketing system. Seats are consistently well detailed and careful choice of street lighting adds to the human scale.

The hierarchy of spatial experiences is also very well handled, and as evidence of increasing awareness of the plight of the handicapped in the community, the use of 'drop kerbs' makes the Centre accessible to the old and disabled.

Bukit Batok Neighbourhood 3 Centre may be an oasis in the HDB domain, but it confidently points the way to an improving environment in Singapore's New Towns.

97

(Overleaf)
The reinterpretation of the traditional five-foot way and its 'appropriation' by shopkeepers as additional display area, makes it a highly successful space. It has a sense of place and the architects have succeeded in creating a delightful stage for the enactment of life's daily drama.

1. Alexander, Christopher. *A Pattern Language.* Oxford University Press. New York. 1977.

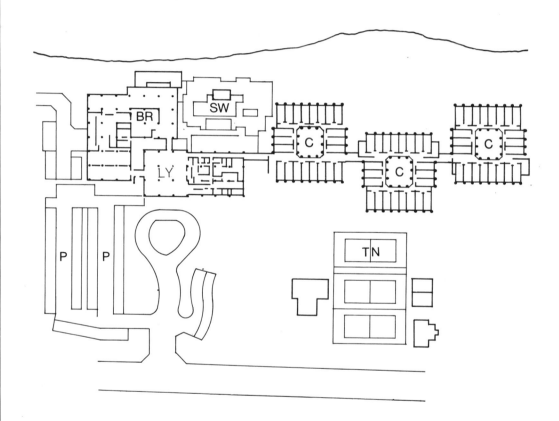

HYATT HOTEL, KUANTAN

The site is long and narrow; sandwiched
between the sea and thickly wooded hills.

BR Bar
C Court
LY Lobby
M Machine Room
ME Main Entrance
P Parking
RS Restaurant
SH Shop
SW Swimming Pool
TN Tennis Court
TR Terrace

HYATT HOTEL, KUANTAN
TELOK CHEMPEDAK BEACH, KUANTAN, MALAYSIA

ARCHITECT: KUMPULAN AKITEK

COMPLETED: 1979

CLIENT
Kuantan Beach Hotel Sdn Bhd

ARCHITECT
Kumpulan Akitek

PROJECT TEAM
Chan Sau Wan, Sonny (Partner-in-charge)
Arnop Nathalang (Project Architect)
Kwok Kum Tong

CONSULTANTS
Structural Engineer
Perunding Bersatu Sdn Bhd
Mechanical and Electrical Engineer
Perunding Bersatu Sdn Bhd
Quantity Surveyor
Juru Ukur Bahan Malaysia
Landscape Architect
Belt Collins and Associates Ltd

MAIN CONTRACTOR
Tab Faiyin Construction Sdn Bhd

The traditional Malay house, together with its later derivative — the colonial bungalow — and the open layout of the kampong, were the sources of reference for Kumpulan Akitek in the design of this 250 bedroom hotel.

Located at Telok Chempedak Beach, approximately 4 kilometres from the centre of Kuantan, the long and narrow site is sandwiched by the South China Sea and thickly wooded hills. Although the site measures 3.6 ha in total, existing planning legislation restricted the architect to just 1.2 ha of the site along a 250 metre shoreline, the remainder being allotted to parking and recreational purposes.

The hotel, operated by the Hyatt International chain, is aimed at the lucrative business-convention and tourist market, and as such, sets out to marry an experience of life in the tropics with the highest standards of comfort of an international hotel.

For this building type, the neo-vernacular architectural language that the designer has adopted is eminently suitable. It has proved successful elsewhere — Geoffrey Bawa has employed the typology in his Triton Hotel in Ahungalla, south of Colombo in Sri Lanka. The Tanjung Jara Beach Hotel and Rantau Abang Visitor's Centre are similar successful projects on the east coast of West Malaysia.

Thus, whilst the guestrooms and some public areas are air-conditioned from a central plant, the main lobby and circulation spaces of the hotel are naturally ventilated. I personally prefer even less air-conditioning though this is an opinion probably not shared by a majority of tourists.

The structure is an *insitu* reinforced concrete frame with brick partition walls. The roofs are timber-framed and covered with locally manufactured tiles — an adaptation of a traditional material. Unlike the Tanjong Jara Hotel which employs traditional techniques, the essence of the timber columns in the traditional Malay kampong house is reinterpreted here in concrete. Hence the building is an example of modern architecture which draws inspiration from regional heritage.[1]

The site constraints determine a low-rise development along a north-south axis. A series of pavilions, linked by open verandahs, take advantage of the beach frontage.

The main reception lobby is an open-sided, double-tiered roofed pavilion of marvellous proportions. Accentuated by strategically placed up-lighters, the pavilion is separated by a reflecting pool from another 'L' shaped pavilion housing the restaurant, bar and function rooms. At a lower level is a coffee house and an outdoor seafood restaurant projecting onto the beach. The guestrooms are contained in three pavilions arranged around landscaped airwells. The focus of the complex is the swimming pool which overlooks the sea.

Both the exterior and interior of the hotel have been landscaped to recreate a lush, luxuriant tropical environment which also minimises radiated heat from hard surfaces.

The Hyatt Kuantan is a valid approach to tropical architecture. It responds to climatic factors with its open pavilions, shaded walkways, pitched roofs, high ceilings and use of balconies. The wide projecting eaves and verandahs of indigenous dwellings provide a model, and being used consistently, ensures visual harmony. Full use is made of local resources such as clay tiles.

Inspiration is drawn from the traditional architecture of east coast Malaysia where buildings are raised on stilts, while the main pavilion has echoes of the two storey wooden *Istana* (palaces) of the early sultans of the region.

There is a search for consistency with the historical context, and the built form seeks to perpetuate indigenous styles.

It fosters cultural continuity, although it is largely for the use of tourists, which therefore raises some difficult ideological issues. The designer has, nevertheless, achieved a commendable quality in the spatial heirarcy and scale of the hotel.

Kumpulan Akitek has succeed in creating a development that fuses past and present — an architecture which is contemporary and yet retains a strong link with the rich heritage of the Malayan Peninsula.

1. Wong Chong Thai, Bobby. Regionalism in Architecture. Unpublished Essay on Regionalism. School of Architecture. National University of Singapore. 1987.

The site constraints determine a low-rise development along a north-south axis. A series of pavilions linked by open verandahs take advantage of the beach frontage.

The main reception lobby is an open sided, double tiered roofed pavilion of exquisite proportions. The essence of the timber columns in the traditional Malay *Istana* is reinterprated here in concrete.

For this building type, the neo-vernacular language that the architect has adopted is eminently suitable. The focus of the project is the swimming pool which has a view of the expansive South China Sea.

102

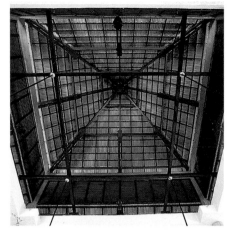

103

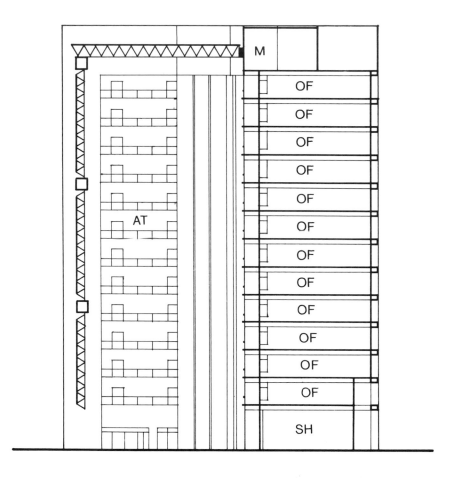

PARKWAY BUILDERS' CENTRE

Section indicating the structure of the naturally ventilated atrium overlooked by offices. Shops and restaurants are located at the first storey, and they are accessed from the covered plaza.

Plan at first storey. The 'L' shaped office block encloses the atrium.

AT Atrium
M Machine Room
OF Office
RS Restaurant
SH Shop

104

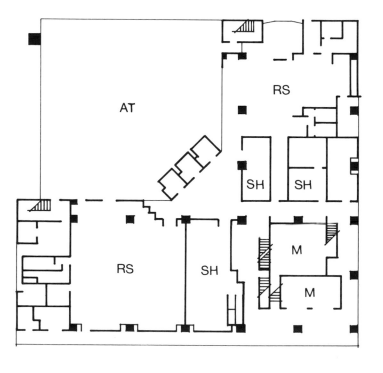

PARKWAY BUILDERS' CENTRE
MARINE PARADE ROAD, SINGAPORE 1543

ARCHITECT: AKITEK TENGGARA

COMPLETED: FEBRUARY 1985

CLIENT
People's Park Development Pte Ltd

ARCHITECT
Akitek Tenggara

PROJECT TEAM
Tay Kheng Soon (Partner-in-charge)
Paul Appasamy (Project Architect)
Patrick Chia (Project Architect)

CONSULTANTS
Engineer
KTP Ho
Quantity Surveyor
Rider, Hunt, Levett and Bailey

MAIN CONTRACTORS
Wendy International
Kwong Kum Sum Cheo

(Overleaf)
The plaza at the base of the atrium is sheltered by a huge 'umbrella' of aluminium and glass. Outdoor eating is an integral part of Singaporean culture and this building gives the ground floor of the private office block 'back to the people'.

This thirteen storey 'L' shaped office block encompasses a soaring naturally ventilated atrium enclosed in a glass-clad, aluminium tube space frame. It is conceptually simple, and yet arguably the most advanced built example in Singapore of a 'tropical high-rise' building. To quote Edwards and Keys, 'It represents one of the few serious attempts in Singapore to produce an exciting, yet functionally responsive solution to the problem of creating office accommodation.'[1]

There is, in the work of Akitek Tenggara, a strong theoretical basis — a search for a Singaporean identity, a tropical modern architecture. In this, Tay Kheng Soon has since 1967 articulated the need to carefully reassess imported models and to search for a Singaporean identity in response to the climate and the plural roots of Singaporean culture. It is hard to deny the soundness of such a proposition when one sees the possibilities demonstrated in this building.

The project is not without its faults. Principally, there is deterioration of some of the materials by corrosion. Stainless steel door frames have not withstood the tropical climate within the atrium, paintwork on the walls of open corridors has adhesion problems and some additional fixings have been added to polished granite cladding to correct earlier fixing problems.

Although these problems are part of the problem of building in a tropical environment, the building is a conceptually challenging one.

The full height atrium is glazed on two sides and at roof level, and there is a series of giant louvres attached to the outer face of the space frame structure. In theory, air is thus drawn in and upwards, naturally ventilating the atrium space. Slight air movement past the open access corridors cuts down further energy requirement. There is thus an attempt to use the tropical climate positively and to save energy unlike the standard office tower solution of air-conditioning which is derived directly from models of skyscrapers in temperate climates. Also, the ubiquitous enclosed atrium, the modern version of which originated 30 degrees north of the Equator in Atlanta, Georgia, is applied everywhere in the tropics without rigorous re-examination of its context.

Three glazed passenger lifts rise out of the sheltered public plaza at the base of the Parkway Builders' Centre. The plaza is arguably the most successful part of the project, accommodating an outdoor dining space which is sheltered yet exposed to cooling breezes. It can also accommodate exhibitions, displays and even stage shows. The single loaded corridors can also serve as viewing galleries.

Despite its material and finishing problems, the building impresses by its clear, confident form and response to its context. Outdoor eating is an integral part of Singaporean culture and yet so few new developments attempt to offer the ground floor to the public. Here is an innovative approach to the problem, in effect giving the ground floor space of a private office block 'back to the people'.

The major test of an architect's theoretical propositions comes when he is faced with a building type that does not lend itself to regional interpretations. A church, a hotel, a cultural or recreational building is far easier to handle than a computer installation, a bank or a high-rise office block.

The high-rise building, with the exception of some 8- to 10-storey adobe buildings in Sana'a, Yemen and pagodas in China, is an invention of the Western world. Asia, Africa and South America came much later than Europe and the USA to high-rise technology.

To quote Ken Yeang, a Malaysian architect 'We require a regionalist alternative to the Modernists flat-surfaced, flat topped, neutral-coloured, modular containers.'[2]

Responding by design to climatic constraints and cultural patterns is the first step towards producing a high-rise alternative architecture relevant to its place and time. Parkway Builders' Centre is an appropriate example of this direction.

1. Edwards, Norman and Keys, Peter. *Singapore. A Guide to Buildings, Streets and Places.* Times Books International, Singapore. 1988.
2. Yeang, Ken. *Land Use, Climate and Architectural Form in Design for High Intensity Development.* PAM and Aga Khan Program at MIT/Harvard. Kuala Lumpur. 1985.

**NANYANG TECHNOLOGICAL INSTITUTE
HALL OF RESIDENCE NO.V**

Section through residential blocks and
pedestrian street showing the intimate
character of the courtyards which are
surrounded by the student rooms.

Nanyang Technological Institute, Hall
of Residence No. V. First storey plan. The
pedestrian street links the four block of
the Hall of Residence with adjoining halls.
At the centre is a public meeting place.

108

BD Bedroom
C Court
CN Conference Room
D Dining
K Kitchen
ME Main Entrance
OF Office
PS Pedestrian Street

st storage
v void

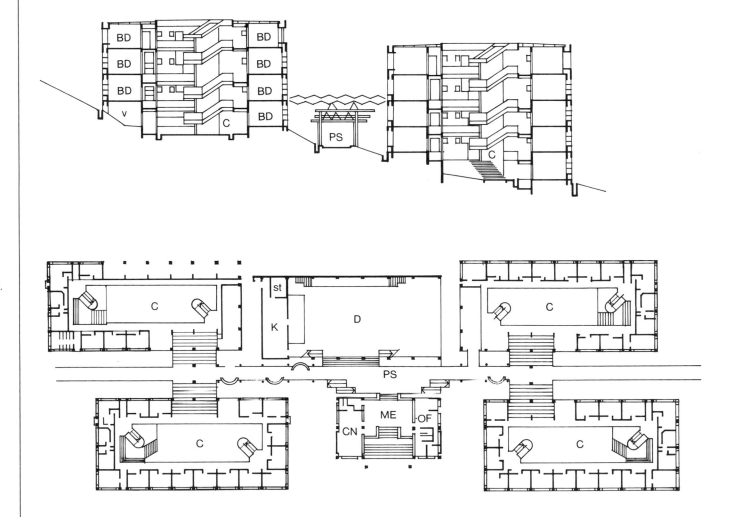

NANYANG TECHNOLOGICAL INSTITUTE HALL OF RESIDENCE NO. V
NANYANG CRESCENT, SINGAPORE 2263

ARCHITECT: AKITEK TENGGARA

COMPLETED: 1989

CLIENT
Nanyang Technological Institute

ARCHITECT
Akitek Tenggara

PROJECT TEAM
Tay Kheng Soon (Partner-in-charge)
Patrick Chia (Project Architect)

CONSULTANTS
Structural Engineer
Houkehua Consulting Engineers
Mechanical and Electrical Engineer
Specs Consultants Pte Ltd
Quantity Surveyor
Rider, Hunt, Levitt and Bailey

MAIN CONTRACTOR
Lee Kim Tah (Pte) Ltd

In this, the latest of their completed projects, Akitek Tenggara affirm their deserved position at the very 'cutting edge' of innovation in Singapore architecture.

The concept of the building is marvellously original, exploring many of the ideas that Tay Kheng Soon, the principal architect of the practice, has enunciated in his essays and applied in his built works.

The idea of outdoor covered space, of shaded linkages, of creating identity, fashioning places for casual encounters, of creating what Norberg-Schultz has called a *genius-loci* (sense of place), are all here.

In short, this building is designed for tropical living and a Singaporean lifestyle — one where people might sit out-of-doors in the evening in shaded courtyards, where living rooms overlook communal spaces; spaces which just as in the kampong, can become the focus of activity. Furthermore, these spaces are of intimate human scale, designed to enclose and foster a sense of belonging in a special community. It is a robust, strongly articulated building, but one which is not at all overpowering.

The form of the hall of residence is deceptively simple. Four rectangular hollow-square blocks each housing 125 students are placed in the four corners of a larger rectangular complex. The remaining two rectangles in the centre of the complex house the multi-purpose covered space and the administration block and master's house.

The linkage route between these six rectangles is a steel space frame which is part glazed and part roofed. The centre of the complex is an area of intense concentration of activities; a focus for all the students. Here, students can sit on concrete curved seats or on the cascade of steps from the entrance. Evocative of the 'Piazza di Spagna' in Rome, this is destined to become a popular meeting node and a landmark of the sprawling campus.

The residential blocks are constructed around a strongly articulated concrete frame, with each module being that of a typical student room. The infill is glazed metal windows set behind the concrete frame to provide partial shade. There is also a deep recess below the windows to allow air to circulate freely into the room. The finish of the concrete frame regrettably does not do justice to the concept. The original specification was for steel shuttering which had to be omitted when heavy foundation costs were incurred on the steeply sloping, narrow site. The compromise detracts from the general standard of building finishes. It is, nonetheless, preferable to the ubiquitous plaster finish that covers many buildings in Singapore. It would be a pity if this building were to suffer the same fate.

The practicalities of student life are tackled in the details. For example, there is a shoe rack outside each student's room door.

The four residential blocks have the same basic configuration. Each has its own central courtyard and is given identity by the panels of bold colours below the windows. The design elements give each block a sense of being a smaller world within the community of the NTI.

There is a sense of grandeur about the entrance. It is memorable, slightly monumental, and yet totally approachable. A curved perspex canopy spans two cantilevered concrete beams, beyond which is a light-filled central space. The effect is that of a rather grand entrance balanced by a sense of permeability and the layering of the interior.

The hall of residence is totally modern, yet it cleverly reinterprets traditional ways of responding to the tropical climate. Lightwells, overhangs, covered walkways, open-to-sky spaces, shaded reveals, all work well within the context of the steeply sloping and restricted site.

The result is a unique and distinctly Singaporean building in the forefront of innovative thinking.

The search for a modern regional architecture is at the heart of current discourse among the intellectual avant garde and concerned practitioners in Asia. It has formed the basis of several fora of ARCASIA (The Architects Regional Council Asia). Tay Kheng Soon is a prominant figure in this on-going dialogue. The NTI hall of residence is a practical enunciation of his ideas on a hybrid Abstract Regionalism which transforms cultural patterns, responds to climatic imperatives and utilises the technology benefits of modernism. It has many lessons for the next generation of architects.

There is a sense of grandeur about the main entrance. It is slightly monumental and yet approachable. The curved perspex canopy spans two cantilevered concrete beams; beyond is a light-filled courtyard. The cascade of steps is destined to become a popular meeting place on the campus.

The idea of a outdoor covered space, of shaded linkages, places where people might sit in the evening and of an intimate human scale are all present within this robust, strongly articulated building.

The centre of the complex is an area of intense concentration of activities. A focus for all the students, it is a grand covered plaza at the intersection of walkways. Cultural patterns and climate are the generators of the built form.

The four residential blocks are each constructed around a courtyard. Each block is given a separate identity by the panels of bold colour used below the windows and along the access balconies.

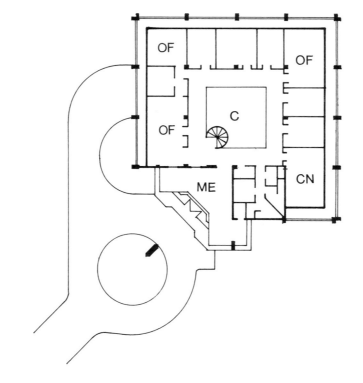

SWISS CHANCERY

Second storey plan. Offices occupy the external wall of a hollow square. A circulation corridor looks into an internal court.

Section. Office windows are well shaded by the overhanging roof.

C Court
CN Conference Room
OF Office
ME Main Entrance
P Parking

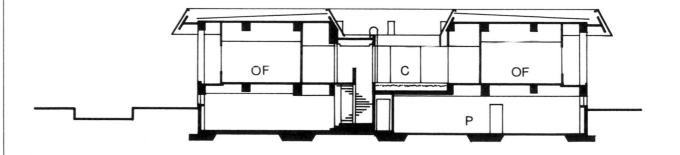

SWISS CHANCERY
SWISS CLUB LINK, SINGAPORE 1128

ARCHITECT: GORDEN BENTON AND ASSOCIATES
and Rolf Kaiser Consulting Architect

COMPLETED: 1987

CLIENT
The Swiss Confederation
represented by the Swiss Federal
Buildings Office

ARCHITECT
Gordon Benton and Associates
in association with R Kaiser Consulting
Architect

PROJECT TEAM
Gordon Benton (Partner-in-charge)
Rolf Kaiser (Consulting Architect)
Amado Pilar (Project Architect)

CONSULTANTS
Structural Engineer
Harris and Sutherland Pte Ltd
Mechanical and Electrical Engineer
J Roger Preston and Partners Pte Ltd
Quantity Surveyor
Partnership International McDonald and
Partners Pte Ltd
Landscape Architect
BCP Far East

MAIN CONTRACTOR
Shimizu Construction Co. Ltd

Think of Switzerland and the images that come to mind are of a relatively small nation committed to quality in design and craftsmanship, and to an independence of thought and action that sets it apart from many of its European neighbours.

Translate that into architecture and it almost exactly sums up the Swiss Chancery in Singapore. Tucked away at the end of Swiss Club Road, the building is beautiful, yet modest and unassuming.

As with the adjoining Swiss Club restoration and extensions (p.60), for which Gordon Benton and Associates were also responsible, the architect's starting point was the physical context — a 0.8 hectare plot of relatively undisturbed jungle.

The success of the contractor in protecting the forest results in a building which, though extensive, sits comfortably within a well established environment.

The brief was for a new Chancery and related staff housing, and a slope of eleven metres across the site gave the architects the opportunity to step the buildings down the face of the hill. The access is from Swiss Club Link.

The plan of the Chancery is very simple. Designed as a square and based on a 5 metre by 5 metre structural grid, it consist of offices around the 20 metre by 20 metre perimeter formed by an internal corridor and a central landscaped court. Below are private car parking spaces and service rooms.

The offices have an atmosphere of calm and quiet efficiency, discreet lighting and some original paintings.

In the reception area, marble, stainless steel and polished granite are the dominant materials. The finishing, as at the junction of walls and ceiling and the perfect alignment of light fittings, is noticeably precise.

The contractor's standards are of the highest order — an achievement which the architects attribute to the contractor's own rigorous site management and comprehension of sophisticated detailing. However, I suspect that it may also reflect on Gordon Benton's own demands for excellence, and those of the consultant architect, Rolf Kaiser.

Throughout, the feeling is of understated, somewhat conservative, good taste. It is certainly modern but is perhaps a little cold for those who prefer a more direct experience of the landscape.

The internal court is a visual delight but it can only be enjoyed from the air-conditioned interior.

Ideally, the relationship between the courtyard and the interior would be more intimate if all the windows opened and simple ceiling fans were used instead of air-conditioning. In practice, however, this would clearly compromise security.

This comment aside, the building is an extremely good attempt to apply the principles of modern functional architecture within tropical climatic constraints. The architects eschew a flamboyant play of form or traditional cliches and have produced a 'modern civic European' image in a tropical setting.

Here, the horizontal emphasis and white rendered finish used externally contrast sharply with the vertical form and lushness of the surrounding vegetation.

The Swiss Chancery is arguably not a tropical building in the sense that it relies entirely upon air-conditioning. The contact with the forest is purely visual and there is no direct contact with the setting nor the opportunity to enjoy the rich, earthy smells of the forest.

This is true, and yet the principles of good design found in the building are still important.

There is shading of the external glazed walls by the large overhanging roof — resulting in a reduction of solar heat gain.

The extensive planting alongside the building, together with the retention of quite a substantial number of forest trees reduces the radiant heat and thus create an equable micro-climate.

Keeping in mind the specific use of the building in a tropical environment is important, for not all uses will lend themselves to the openness of traditional models. Many buildings, such as the Swiss Chancery, will require air-conditioning for a stable internal temperature and security.

Just as Switzerland is a peaceful and prosperous enclave, discreetly protecting the anonymity of its foreign bank accounts in a beautiful wooded country, so the Swiss Chancery rejects the high profile of a city centre location and functions from its forest setting, presenting a slightly enigmatic face to the public.

The Swiss Chancery rejects the high profile of a city centre location and functions from its forest setting, presenting a slightly enigmatic face to the public.

The internal landscaped courtyard can be enjoyed from the air-conditioned interior. Security considerations clearly compromise a more open plan arrangement.

The architects eschewed a flamboyant play of form or traditional cliches and have produced a modern civic image in the midst of a tropical setting.

114

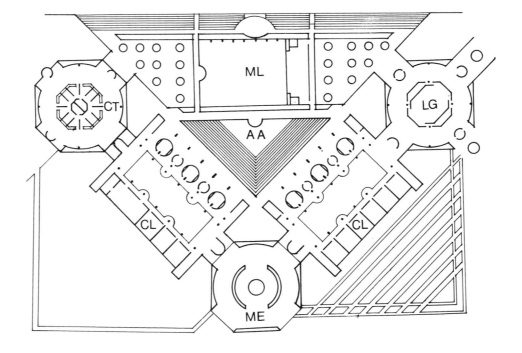

TAMPINES JUNIOR COLLEGE

116 First storey plan indicating the generous shaded circulation space and the built form which encloses an amphitheatre.

Section through the main entrance, the amphitheatre and the multi-purpose hall.

AA Assembly Area
CL Classroom
CT Canteen
LG Lounge
ME Main Entrance
ML Multi-purpose Room/Hall

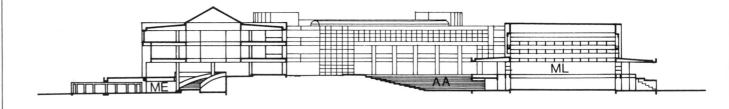

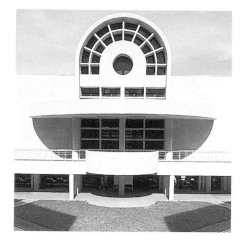

TAMPINES JUNIOR COLLEGE
TAMPINES AVENUE 9, SINGAPORE 1852

ARCHITECT: P AND T ARCHITECTS

COMPLETED: 1987

CLIENT
Ministry of Education

ARCHITECT
P and T Architects

PROJECT TEAM
Alan KG Low (Partner-in-charge)
Sern Vithespongse (Project Architect)
Choy Meng Yew (Project Architect)

CONSULTANTS
Structural Engineer
Public Works Department
Mechanical and Electrical Engineer
Public Works Department
Quantity Surveyor
Public Works Department
Landscape Architect
Parks and Recreation Department
P and T Architects

MAIN CONTRACTOR
Metrobilt Construction Pte Ltd

Tampines Junior College is one of the very recent Junior College buildings which seems set to achieve the aim of creating schools buildings with a distinct identity. It is one which the student can respond to with pride, which fosters a strong loyalty, and provides an atmosphere in which individuality can be nourished alongside a broader communal responsibility. It is instantly identifiable as a school and is recognisable as a landmark when seen against the backcloth of public housing from the Tampines Expressway.

The complex is made of two rectangular blocks located between three octagonal node points which form a triangle. The rectangular blocks contain classrooms and laboratories, whilst the octagonal node buildings house the administration, library, lecture theatres and the canteen.

Bisecting the angle made by the two rectangular blocks is the assembly hall, squash courts and an air-rifle range. Over the hall is a barrel vault, the ends of which are glazed; it is this feature which give the building its distinct profile adding to the landmark qualities of the school. The sides of the triangle embrace, both visually and metaphorically, the sports arena.

The architect set out to create visual impact by building the school on an elevated platform. This, and the geometric forms, give the school a formal appearance — an image which is enhanced by the monochromatic palette of pale grey and green used for finishes throughout. The colonnaded forecourt and the podium, reminiscent of classical temple structures, enhances this formality.

This slight monumentality is offset by an openness (which suggests accessibility) under and between the forms. Despite the colonnade the entrance to the school is somewhat uncelebrated.

The Assembly Hall is cleverly placed to give a dramatic backdrop to both an outdoor amphitheatre and the school running track.

In the detailed resolution of the building, the architects have successfully integrated natural ventilation and sunshading for classrooms and laboratories. Facilities for handicapped children are incorporated at first storey level.

The design is firmly rooted in modernist precedence rejecting traditional form, cultural references and applied decoration.

The practice's approach could be termed Regional Modernism — combining a functional modernist approach to planning with an attempt to respond to the climate of Singapore.

One measure of this is the amount of shaded circulation space provided — literally 50 per cent of the total covered area. Thus, a cool modern architecture with its clarity of planning, is imbued with an openness and tropical informality which encourages interaction.

My only criticism is that there is nevertheless a lack of exuberance and spontaneity — the symmetrical layout and the expression of order in the building suggests a degree of conformity and control. This, however, is perhaps not at all inappropriate to the creation of a disciplined approach to learning.

All buildings have an ability to evoke responses in the observer and the user. My reading of the semantic properties of the built form is that it reflects an emphasis on technology, the sciences and rationality, elements essential for a country which must stay in the forefront of commerce and industry in order to survive and prosper.

It is a rhetorical question, but can the same environment stimulate and nurture the arts: literature, drama and music? This arguably requires a more tactile information-rich environment which has more variegated forms.

Architectural forms can reflect and be supportive of a pedagogy, but it can equally stimulate and shape the attitudes of students and teachers alike.

One further observation is that seeing all the facilities of the school locked and unused on a Sunday afternoon, one wonders if the building could form even more of a focus if its facilities were available for the local community. But this is not architectural criticism.

The building is an impressive example of a new commitment to quality in education.

It forms a dignified and thoroughly modern crucible for the nurturing of young minds and the stimulation of innovative teaching.

The Assembly Hall provides a dramatic backdrop to both the outdoor amphitheatre and the school running track. There is arguably a lack of exuberance and spontaneity in the form, yet the symmetrical layout and the expression of order suggests a degree of conformity and control which may not be inappropriate to a disciplined approach to learning.

The school is built on an elevated platform. This, and the geometric forms, give the school a formal appearance, an image which is enhanced by the monochromatic palette of pale grey and green used for finishes throughout. The colonaded forecourt enhances the formality.

The school is constantly identifiable as a landmark when set against the backcloth of public housing. Over the assembly hall is a barrel vault. It is this feature which gives the building its distinct profile.

119

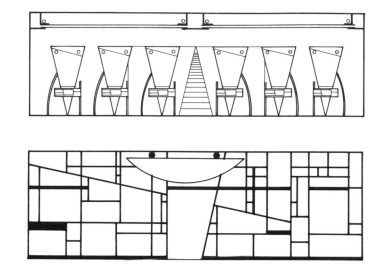

KIMARIE

Section.

Elevation to Raffles Boulevard. The salon's front facade is a strong composition in black lines and primary colours.

Bird's eye view of the hairdressing salon.

Plan. A semi-circular lobby and reception counter lead to a central axis terminating in a granite triangle on the rear wall.

120

L Living
LG Lounge
RC Reception
SL Salon
SM Shopping Mall
WS Washroom

d display

SM

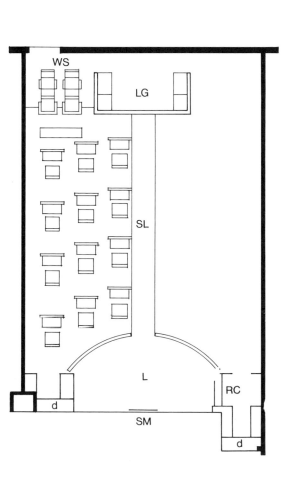

KIMARIE

6 RAFFLES BOULEVARD, #03-303/304
SINGAPORE 0103

ARCHITECT: MANOP ARCHITECTS

COMPLETED: 1987

CLIENT
Kimarie Salon and Beauty Training Centre

ARCHITECT
Manop Architects

**PARTNER-IN-CHARGE AND
PROJECT ARCHITECT**
Manop Phakinsri

CONSULTANTS
Mechanical and Electrical Engineer
Technic Consultant

MAIN CONTRACTOR
Woodrise Interior

The architect draws inspiration for this hairdressing salon from many sources, but the resulting effect is entirely unique.

The entrance facade from the shopping mall is a curious hybrid; the strong composition in black metal angles reminds one immediately of a Piet Mondrian painting — especially since the primary red, blue and yellow used characterised the painter's work, particularly from 1920 onwards.

However, immediately one settles for this interpretation, one's eyes are drawn to two display windows, both of which have a surreal quality. Ordinary items of everyday use in the salon — a circular brush, a pair of scissors — become *objet d'art*, arranged on a bed of fine sand in front of white paper clouds. The image is distinctly that of Max Ernst or Salvador Dali.

The 'boat shaped' shop sign, once again, stirs one's memory, unfolding distinct echoes of Hans Hollein's Juwelier Schullin in Vienna's Kohlmarket[1]. In fact, Manop Phakinsri studied for a short period during the mid-1980s in the Austrian architect's design studio at the Domus Academy in Milan.

What might become a chaotic assortment of visual stimulii from so many sources is tightly controlled by the geometry of the glazing bars of the shop window. Dynamism is introduced into the composition by the clever tilting of just one transome and one mullion away from the orthogonal grid.

Step inside, and the designer leads us to a semi-circular lobby. A curved wall, slightly above head height and executed in glass blocks, is echoed by concentric bands of black and grey marble. Subtle diffused lighting and strategic spotlights give an image of youthful fashion, but the designer chairs in black steel indicate it is definitely up-market. Equally elegant is the reception counter of the salon.

Penetrate further on the central axis and the alternate black and grey bands of granite terminate in a triangle on the rear wall of the salon.

Two heavily studded columns finished in black steel give another brief resonance of the architecture of Shin Takamatsu — particularly his Pharoah Dental Office project in Kyoto, Japan.

Manop Phakinsri is successful in organising the working area of the salon. The ceiling and concealed lighting are well detailed, the individual cutting tables with triangular mirrors are exquisite sculptured objects displayed on a green tiled floor. The decision to have individual work stations is a distinct change from the purely functional arrangement where mirrors line the two parallel walls of a shop unit. However, the area is slightly cluttered — this being an economic decision not in the hands of the designer.

Perhaps the only disappointment is the salon chairs — a standard product which suggests there is a fortune to be made by the one who takes the initiative to update standard hairdressing furniture design.

Kimarie is essentially about fashion, and the designer's job was to create an image of elegant precision. This, Manop does with wit and style, showing the two qualities which are a reflection of the man. The architect moved his office to Chiangmai in mid-1988 and now commutes regularly between that city and Bangkok.

He should find himself very much at home in the Thai capital, for Thailand too is going through a synthesis of its long and rich tradition with the architectural forms of Western origin.

The results are sometimes eclectic and often more bizarre than are seen in Singapore. One can find a Greek Temple structure atop a modern apartment block (Jareemart Mansion) and a similar hybrid language for a major office block (Amarin Plaza) in Bangkok's business district. There is a bank built in the form of a robot (Bank of Asia — architect, Sumet Jumsai) and another office with a Lego-like appearance.

This gives some measure of the stylistic confusion that exists in another Asian society which is in rapid transition. Like Singapore, Thailand is seeking to synthesise the tenets of modernism and tradition and define its own original and new architectural identity.

1. Loo Kok Hoo. Unpublished Essay. Architectural Criticism. School of Architecture. National University of Singapore. 1988.

The individual cutting tables with triangular mirrors are exquisite sculptured objects. The usual salon arrangement is rejected in favour of a layout which stresses the individual image of the client.

The central axis of the salon — alternate bands of black and grey granite — terminates in a triangle on the rear wall. The floor pattern is echoed by a semi-circular glass block wall. The architect takes his inspiration from many sources, but the resulting effect is entirely unique.

The 'boat-shaped' shop sign has distinct echoes of the Juwelier Schullin shop in Vienna's Kohlmarket.

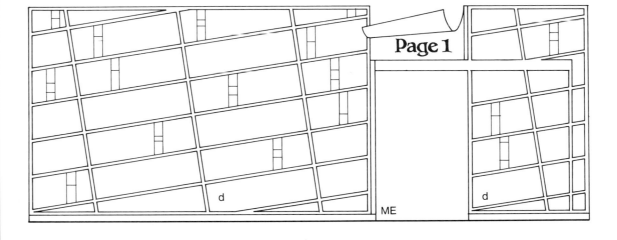

PAGE ONE

Elevation to Raffles Boulevard.

124 Plan showing the dynamic juxtaposition of
display elements of this unique bookshop.

Page One. A bird's eye view of the interior.

ME Main Entrance
OF Office
SH Shop
SM Shopping Mall

d display

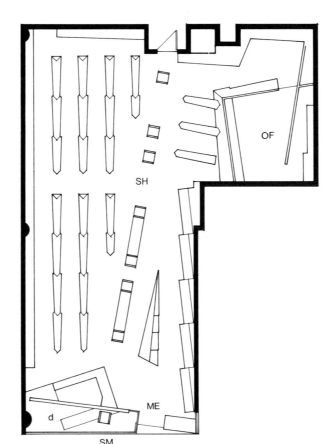

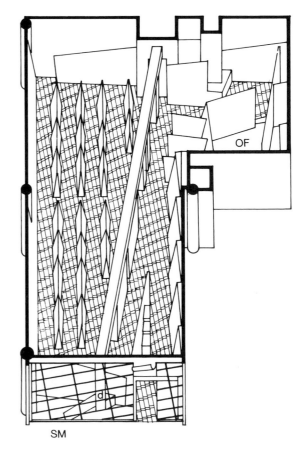

PAGE ONE
6, RAFFLES BOULEVARD, #03-128
SINGAPORE 0103

ARCHITECT: MANOP ARCHITECTS

COMPLETED: 1987

CLIENT
Page One — The Designer Bookshop

ARCHITECT
Manop Architects

**PARTNER-IN-CHARGE AND
PROJECT ARCHITECT**
Manop Phakinsri

CONSULTANT
Mechanical and Electrical Engineer
Technic Consultant

MAIN CONTRACTORS
Francis Interior and Woodrise Interior

Very little new ground has been explored in the design of shop interiors in Singapore in the last decade. There is no shortage of designer boutiques with marble and deep pile carpets, but really memorable interiors in shopping centres are few and far between.

Manop Architects have added to this very short list the remarkably innovative design for Page One Bookshop in Marina South Mall. The immediate and somewhat startling discovery is that all the book shelves slope and there is hardly a horizontal surface throughout the shop!

It is a clever device to give the interior a unique quality and, though it may give the impression of being impractical, it clearly is not. Think about it: to read the title of a book standing spine up on a shelf, one has to twist one's neck at an awkward angle. So there is no lack of good sense in tilting the shelves. But this is not the real reason, it is basically a designer's device to create a unique and surprising effect.

The shopfront picks up the theme of the interior. A series of transoms at the same spacing as the internal shelf, slope down from right to left. The Page One sign is quite small and shows a sparkling touch of wit; it is a clever metaphor of an opening page of a book.

Inside, the floor is black slate laid at an angle to the main thrust of the space. Specialist books on design, art, photography, graphics and architecture are shown full face. They provide colour and interest,

and become a major element in the overall design of the interior.

It is a rare shop design that will stand out in a busy shopping mall. Many employ expensive materials and an impressive array of spotlights to little effect, but Page One is unique; the facade draws in the public curious to explore its interior.

It is a design of immense skill and combines the art of commercial packaging with architecture to

startling effect. It explores new frontiers in shop design in Singapore.

Manop Phakinsri is a Thai architect who has always brought wit into his design. He came to Singapore in 1970 and worked with Design Partnership and then, DP Architects. He started his own practice in 1986 and he returned to his native Thailand just in 1988.

There is hardly a horizontal surface throughout the shop. All the book shelves slope, a device that has some practical purpose but is primarily a visual strategy to create a dynamic and unusual interior.

The Page One sign is small and witty — an opening page of a book. The shop window fenestration reflects the interior theme with a series of sloping transoms.

There is an increasing recognition in Singapore of the importance of excellent commercial and industrial design. It is fitting that a shop which sells books on these subjects displays them with flair.

It is a rare shop design that stands out in a busy shopping mall. Page One is unique — the facade attracts all passer-bys, especially the committed artists and designers.

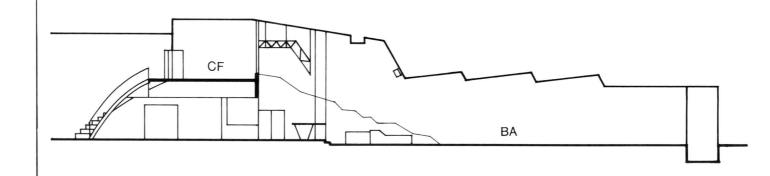

TAPS

Section. Taps Cafe and the Bowling Alley.

Mezzanine floor plan.

128

BA Bowling Alley
BR Bar
CF Cafe
DC Discotheque
F Foyer
K Kitchen

f female
m male
st storage

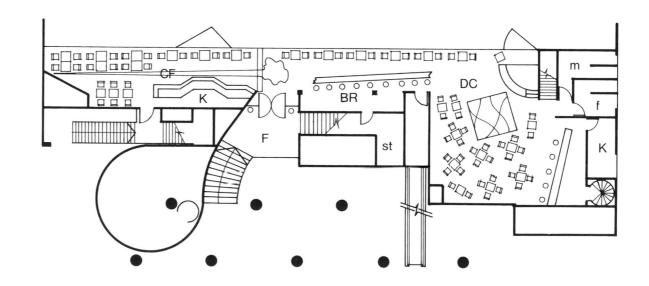

TAPS CAFE
ORCHARD CINEMA, GRANGE ROAD
SINGAPORE 0923

ARCHITECT: TANGGUANBEE ARCHITECTS

COMPLETED: 1987

CLIENT
Orchard Bowling (Pte) Ltd

ARCHITECT
TangGuanBee Architects

**PARTNER-IN-CHARGE AND
PROJECT ARCHITECT**
Tang Guan Bee

MAIN CONTRACTOR
Chuan Leong Construction and
Renovation Contractor

Wit requires a mastery of language, a sharp awareness of the current vogue and a sense of timing. To make an architectural joke is equally demanding; it has to be self assured, delivered with a relaxed confidence and striking exactly the right note. Too obvious and it will fall flat.

Taps is an architectural 'one liner' and architect Tang Guan Bee demonstrates that he can go beyond the obvious and the utilitarian to produce a design that is very witty.

The cafe is approached from the decidely plebeian foyer of the Orchard Cinema which highlights the irony. After ascending a short flight of stairs, one steps through a time warp into a surreal world, half of which is a snack bar, the other half a dark, dimly lit discotheque. A second irony is that the place is peopled not by designer-clothed sophisticates but by a young crowd, mostly teenagers who frequent the bowling alley on the ground floor of the building and the cinema.

The cafeteria overlooks the bowling alley and utilises a panoramic glazed window left by the previous tenant. Strands of neon tubes — yellow, pink, green and blue, hang from the ceiling. Small spotlights are set into common household taps suspended on steel conduits from the ceiling — hence the name Taps. More taps appear elsewhere, in equally improbable roles: as a front door handle and as the mounting for a microphone on the disc jockey's console.

Given just three weeks to design the project and a further three for the contractor to complete the on-site work, the architect was allowed a freedom that a normal programme would not permit.

The result is pure theatre with the spontaneity of an art installation. Tang Guan Bee approached each design decision with the question 'Why not?' instead of the more rational 'Why?'.

The materials used are a collage of hy-rib metal lath, perforated metal sheets, steel cables, neon lights, terrazzo, raw brick work, plaster and fragments of tiles. As with his other architectural works (11 Institution Hill and Mandalay Terrace Housing) the architect shows a painterly technique in his use of colour and juxtaposition of elements. The mood of the cafe is projected into the bowling alley with the use of these same materials on the side walls of the bowling alley.

In the disco-cum-lounge area, everything is black and the contrast is striking. All the furniture, with the exception of the chairs, are designed by the architect and has been said to 'bring to mind the tortured metal and glass designs of avant garde London furniture designers like Ron Arad'.[1]

Taps is a major experiment for Tang Guan Bee who readily admits that the fast track programme freed him from conventional restraints and allowed him to explore concepts he would not normally have considered. It allowed his artistic inclinations full scope as revealed in the snack bar where there is a gay profusion of pastel purple and yellow paint and colourful plastic chairs. At one end of the bar, a black mannequin sits atop a bright yellow cube. On the floor, a curious triangular path of broken ceramic tiles ends up in a wavy patch by the front entrance. Tang, rather tongue-in-cheek, explains this as "flowing water ending in a puddle!".

Taps will undoubtedly 'date' quickly — the meaning that might be inferred from this is that Singapore has reached a stage in its development when 'planned obsolescence' is acceptable. The joke will fade and be replaced by another in the 'throw-away' manner described by Alvin Toffler in his book, *Future Shock*.

For the present, it is fun. Though it may be that in Milan or New York it would already be a little dated, this is architecture *in Singapore*, and it is refreshingly happy, delightfully irreverent and totally lacking in self-consciousness. Tang has been quoted as saying that "Singapore does not lack good designers, but suffers from a poverty of high quality materials and technology." The Cathay Organisation have put their trust in one of Singapore's creative designers who has responded to his brief in a daring and innovative manner, giving his client a popular outlet which is crowded with youthful habitues.

129

1. *Interior Quarterly*. Singapore, September/November 1988

Taps appear in many improbable situations; as the front door handle and the mounting for the microphone on the disc jockey's console.

Strands of neon tubes; yellow, pink, green and blue hang from the ceiling. Small spotlights are set into common household taps suspended on a steel conduct from the ceiling — hence the name Taps.

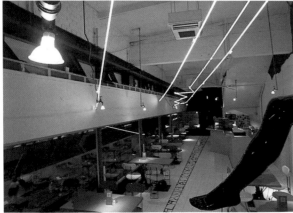

The materials used are a collage of hy-rib metal lath, perforated metal sheets, steel cables, neon lights, terrazzo, raw brick work, plaster and fragments of tiles.
At one end of the bar, a black mannequin sits atop a bright yellow cube; on the floor, a curious path of broken ceramic tiles ends up in a wavy patch by the entrance. The architect, tongue-in-cheek, explains this as 'flowing water ending in a puddle!'

CENTRAL MARKET, KUALA LUMPUR

Second storey plan. The 7.8 metre height
of the building allowed the second floor to
be inserted between the existing columns.

Section.

132 **AT** Atrium
D Dining
E Exhibition
FD Food Stall
OF Office
RC Reception
RS Restaurant
SH Shop
SM Shopping Mall

h hawker stalls

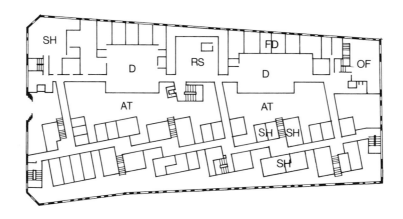

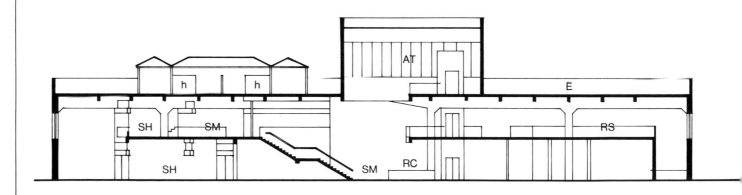

CENTRAL MARKET, KUALA LUMPUR
JALAN HANG KASTURI
KUALA LUMPUR, MALAYSIA

ARCHITECT: WILLIAM LIM ASSOCIATES
in association with Chen Voon Fee of
Architectural Consulting Services and Muhaimin Abdullah

COMPLETED: 1986

CLIENT
Harti-Bumi Sdn Bhd/Lanro Sdn Bhd

ARCHITECT
William Lim Associates
In association with Architectural
Consulting Services (KL)

PROJECT TEAM
William SW Lim (Partner-in-charge)
Chen Voon Vee (Partner-in-charge)
Carl G Larson (Partner-in-charge)
Mildred Cheok (Project Architect)
Beh Ngiap Kim (Project Manager)
Cheong Yew Kuan

CONSULTANTS
Structural Engineer
Ranhill Bersekutu Sdn Bhd
Mechanical and Electrical Engineer
Ranhill Bersekutu Sdn Bhd
Quantity Surveyor
Yong Dan Mohamad Faiz Sdn Bhd

MAIN CONTRACTOR
Tetuan Syarikat Siah Brothers
Trading Sdn Bhd

There are strong ties between architects in Singapore and in Peninsula Malaysia. Indeed, many practices have offices in both countries. William Lim and Chen Voon Fee were founding partners of the Malayan Architects Co-Partnership in 1960, and two decades after they went their separate ways after the dissolution of the practice, they collaborated in the restoration and adaptive reuse of Kuala Lumpur's Central Market.

I have included this project in this book for two reasons. Firstly, it illustrates how the early roots of innovation have blossomed. Secondly, the thrust of Singapore's conservation efforts has been in shophouse buildings, but there is a wealth of warehouses along Clarke Quay and Robertson Quay which await the type of flair that turned Kuala Lumpur's old market into a thriving cultural heart for the city.

The Central Market was designed in 1936 by engineer and architect TY Lee just downriver from the confluence of the Gombak and Klang rivers — the landing place of the city's founding fathers. Art deco and renaissance baroque styles influenced the design. There is a hint of Egyptian style which, it has been said, was inspired by the discovery of Tutan Khamen's tomb in 1922[1].

Central Market is close to the major banks, and is accessible from the major bus stations and the railway station. A group of 23 old shop-houses, deemed unworthy of preservation, were demolished to create parking space for cars and a promenade along the river bank.

The building is a single-storey, trapezoidal box measuring 120 metres by 60 metres. The 7.8 metre height allowed a mezzanine floor to be inserted and the sturdy structure permitted a third level of shops to be built on the roof.

No two facades are alike, but there are strong unifying features. The original doorways are prominent, the fenestration follows a rhythmic pattern and a strong moulded frieze runs round the facade at roof level.

The architects have capitalised on the huge space, large enough, it is said, to hold a football pitch.

The designers have eschewed the idea of creating just another shopping complex, instead, they have consciously striven for a sense of openness, movement, intimacy and colour, with shops arranged in clusters as free-standing pavilions. These clusters are arranged on either side and at an angle to the main axis. This is in response to the splay of the building.

Stairs in each of the two-storey pavilions lead to the second storey and three bridges which provide links across the central mall. A hydraulic passenger lift and the main staircase are located in the central atrium space. One hundred shops are provided, none bigger than 60 square metres, and 88 small kiosks, rented out on a daily basis, ensure a rich mix of shops, thus avoiding the ploy of locating 'anchor' tenants.

If criticism can be levelled at the scheme, it is that despite the architect's best intentions to create a dialectic relationship between the new 'temporary' interior structures and the old 'permanent' shell, the dynamism is dissipated. This is perhaps because the structure for these secondary elements is itself so strongly articulated, and the mezzanine floors are tied to the peripheral walls.[2]

However, the introduction of a barrel vault at right angles to the skylit central mall provides both a focus to the building and re-orientates it back to the river and the outdoor public space.

Originally, the Market was not to be air-conditioned. The coloured Calorex glass reduced solar heat gain and relying on natural ventilation, it was possible to achieve six air changes per hour. However, strong resistance by the developer resulted in air-conditioners being installed.

The Market appears to be successful with an ever changing kaleidescope of visitors: school children, office workers, tourists. Its critics would say that it does not have the spontaneity and vigour of South Street Seaport or Fisherman's Wharf, that there are too many restrictions on art forms, on busking and experimental theatre. This may be debatable but what is certain is that Central Market shows how old forms can be used for new activities.

1. Tan Guat Hoon. 'Central Market – Malaysia's own Covent Garden', *Living Magazine*. Singapore. March 1987.
2. Yip Yuen Hong. Unpublished essay. School of Architecture. National University of Singapore. 1987.

133

There is a hint of Egyptian influence in the art deco and baroque market. It has been said that this was inspired by the discovery of Tutan Khamen's tomb in 1922. In 1936, when T Y Lee designed the original building, there were obvious parallels with the present day, when international styles mix freely with the vernacular to produce hybrid architecture.

The architects have consciously created a feeling of openness, movement and colour. It is a bazaar-like atmosphere with shops, painted in strong primary colours, grouped in clusters as free-standing pavilions.

The metamorphosis of the old building is a model of commercial conservation. It has brought life back to the river bank near the confluence of the Gombak and the Klang. This was the landing place of the city founders, and the placement of the building thus helps to establish the cultural continuity of Malaysia's capital.

The introduction of a barrel vault across the market at right angles to the central mall provides a focus and re-orientates the market back to the river. A hydraulic passenger lift and the main staircase are located in the central atrium space.

HOUSE , CAIRNHILL ROAD

The plan and section of a design which
achieves what only the best conservation
work can — a stimulating relationship
between the old and new.

136 **B** Bathroom
BD Bedroom
D Dining
F Foyer
FM Family Room
K Kitchen
L Living
LA Loggia
PA Patio
S Study
U Utility

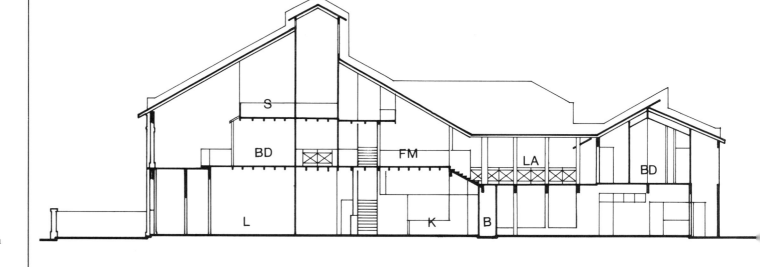

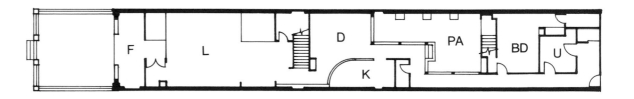

HOUSE, CAIRNHILL ROAD
SINGAPORE 0922

ARCHITECT: DP ARCHITECTS

COMPLETED: 1985

ARCHITECT
DP Architects Pte Ltd

PROJECT TEAM
Chan Sui Him (Partner-in-charge)
Victor Loh Chee Seng (Project Architect)
Manop Phakinsri

CONSULTANTS
Structural Engineer
Engineering Design Partnership
Landscape Architect
DP Architects Pte Ltd

MAIN CONTRACTOR
Everstrong Building Services

Viewed from the outside, this house with its forecourt decorated with original unglazed Malaccan tiles, looks very little different from its neighbours in the street of terrace houses. It certainly gives very little indication of the change that the interior has undergone.

The first hint that changes have been made is apparent when one reaches the porch framed by a grand arched lintel. The original door to the house has been removed and one now enters by turning 90 degrees right, through a small lobby. This is not a casual decision, but the logic is not immediately apparent.

Stepping into the living room beyond, where the original tiled floor is retained, one finds an infill strip of concrete where the crosswall used to be. Again, the reason for this unfinished look is not immediately apparent. However, one is faintly aware that this marks the location of an element of the old interior which has now disappeared. An imprint has been left on the floor, and the architect has deliberately not attempted to disguise the fact.

The staircase which was formerly situated below the ridge line has been moved slightly further back on the plan. The former stairwell is opened as a void to the ridge.

Moving beyond the stair, and still at first storey, one enters the dining area. Daylight floods into the semi-darkened interior through a large window which presents a view of the garden beyond. A corridor leads around the perimeter of the garden to a new extension that has been built at the rear part of the property.

Retracing one's steps to the staircase, and ascending to the second storey, more curious details catch the eye. At the half landing is a balcony which overlooks the centre lightwell. Immediately opposite this is a window — inside the house; it has a small pitched roof complete with traditional roof tiles.

The rationale suddenly becomes clear. The architect has orchestrated a narrative of opposites, of Yin and Yang. We see that the outside is brought inside and external details used internally. It dawns on the observer that as one progresses through the house, there is constant dialogue between old and new. The cornices which originally supported the ceiling below the roof space are retained, even though there is no longer a ceiling. The bare brickwork that was in the roof space is also kept and is now part of a new study. One would have expected it to be neatly plastered. Elsewhere, where ceiling joists have been removed, the holes are not filled but are left as recesses. These are constant reminders of what the house was.

To heighten the dialogical relationship, there are high-tech steel balustrades in bright green.

This is an intellectual exercise but one which is thoroughly intriguing; for this is a reflection of the duality in Chinese culture. The mark of the wall on the first storey floor is now explainable. The manner in which new walls never join the old, but stop slightly short so that new and existing do not join,

is part of the same complex theme.

Even the turning of the front door is now apparent as a response to geomancy. The door, in its former position, faces a minor 'T' junction and is considered unlucky, but also by turning the door, it breaks with the traditional hierarchy.

The skilful manipulation of visual imagery extends further to the master bedroom where the architect creates 'a house within a house'. The original balcony overlooking Cairnhill Road is retained, and in a gesture of deference to its neighbours, the designer retains the modest, even slightly decorative, window grills when others might have been tempted to make a statement of defiance to conventional taste.

At the rear of the house, across the raised garden and accessed via the first storey corridor or the second storey loggia, is a four roomed extension designed in such a way that it can be used as part of the main house or, conceivably, as a separate apartment with rear access.

DP Architects show considerable inventiveness in this intriguing adaptation of the original form. It achieves what only the best conservation work can — a stimulating dialectic relationship between the old and the new. The resolution of past and present, of difference and similarity with equal force. It is a microcosm of the dialogue between modernism and tradition and is to be preferred to either a direct rupture with the past or a weak pastiche of tradition.

The architect has orchestrated a narrative of opposites, of Yin and Yang. The outside is brought inside and external details used internally. A window inside the house has a pitched roof with traditional roof tiles.

There is throughout the house a duality reflecting Chinese culture. Set against the rustic brickwork — an echo of the old construction — is a high-tech steel balustrade.

The entrance to the house has been turned through 90 degrees. In its former position, it faced a 'T' junction and this was considered unlucky because of its adverse placement according to Chinese geomancy.

Throughout this house, there exists a stimulating dialectic relationship between old and new, past and present, of difference and similarity played out with equal force. It is an interesting dialogue between modernism and tradition.

At the rear of the house, accessed by the first storey corridor or the second storey loggia, is a four room extension. It is designed in such a way that it can be used as part of the main house or as a separate apartment. It fits well with the traditional Chinese concept of a two- or three-generation family dwelling.

139

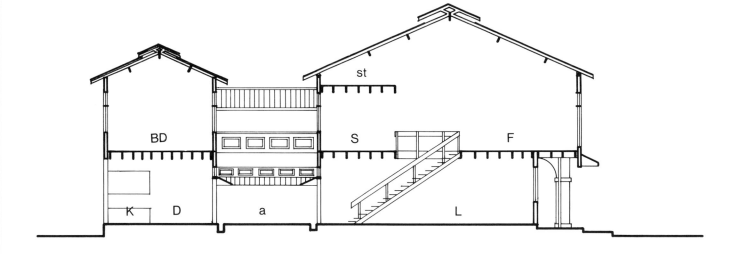

NO. 26 EMERALD HILL ROAD

Section.

First storey plan.

BD Bedroom
D Dining
F Foyer
K Kitchen
L Living
S Study

a airwell
st storage

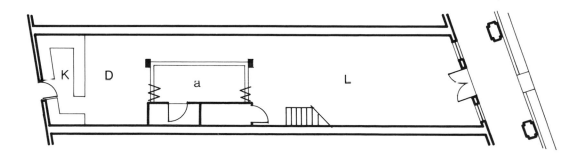

26 EMERALD HILL ROAD
SINGAPORE 0922

ARCHITECT: PAUL TSAKOK

COMPLETED: 1982

ARCHITECT
Paul Tsakok

CONSULTANT
Structural Engineer
Houkehua Consulting Engineers

MAIN CONTRACTOR
Ann Seng Construction Pte Ltd

The growing interest in urban conservation is reflected in recent government policies and private initiatives. It owes much to the early pioneering work of individual entrepreneurs and architects. Historians, Lee Kip Lin[1], Jon Lim and Dr Evelyn Lip[2] have also been instrumental in bringing to the attention of the wider public the valuable architectural heritage, especially in the 'humble' shophouse, a building type imported into many parts of South-east Asia from Southern China.

No. 26 Emerald Hill is the third such conservation project carried out by Paul Tsakok, and it shows the gradual development of a thesis. It is also the one that has been least modified since its completion, and therefore, a model of the architect's personal approach to adaptation of the traditional shophouse.

At a time when there was a great deal of prejudice against these old shophouses, Paul Tsakok expressed his faith in this vernacular townhouse by adapting No. 20 Saunders Road for his own use. It is not too dramatic to say that but for these pioneering efforts, much more of Singapore's built heritage might have been lost. Building on this early experience, Tsakok subsequently remodelled the interiors of Nos. 23 and 26 Emerald Hill.

There is a similarity in the architect's approach to all three examples. The cross walls forming the front room of the houses have been removed, as are the 'L' shaped staircase up to the second storey.

In No. 26, as in the earlier buildings, a straight flight of stairs is then introduced against one of the party walls from first to second storey. The original entrance is retained and one enters straight from the five-foot way into the reception room. The absence of a lobby conforms with the original layout.

Where the cross wall and staircase once stood is now a full height volume to the ridge of the roof. This is a stunning vertical space which is perhaps best appreciated in No. 26 where the proportions and quantity of light appear most effectively balanced. In each of his designs, Tsakok develops a handrail and balustrade detail using mild steel uprights, a hardwood timber rail, glass panels and tensioned wire.

At the rear of the first storey is a kitchen cum dining area; a beautifully detailed and immensely practical space separated from the living and reception area by a narrow but well proportioned open-to-sky light-well. It is a rapturous experience dining here during a tropical thunderstorm as I did in 1984, and having ones conversation accompanied by the crash of thunder and the sound of rainfall. Sunlight and rain are used to good effect rather than being negated as in so many modern air-conditioned buildings.

This house differs from the two earlier examples of Tsakok's work in that subsequent owners and tenants have remained faithful to the original intention of an open plan. In both of his earlier designs, modifications have been introduced to partition and air-condition bedroom space.

In No. 26, there is only one huge double bedroom at the rear, accessed via an open 'loggia' that looks down on the open courtyard. This is of course somewhat restrictive; ideal for a business couple as a *pied-a`-terre* but not so practical for a family — though there is a loft which could be used as a children's garret.

Some owners and their architects in Emerald Hill have remained faithful to the original plans, with only minimal intervention. Others, such as Tsakok take the view that conservation need not be so restrictive. The external facade responds to the scale and ambience of the adjoining street, but inside the building, major structural changes have been made.

In its capability for an infinite variety of internal modifications, the shophouse is not unlike the ubiquitous Georgian or Victorian terrace house in Britain, built for an age of large families and numerous servants, now often adapted into a single luxurious dwelling or into multi-occupation apartments.

The shophouse has similarly shown itself capable of constant adaptive reuse and this typology, and its reinterpretation into a modern form, is worthy of further exploration by both the practising architect and academics alike.

141

1. Lee Kip Lin. *Emerald Hill Road.* National Museum, Singapore. 1984.
2. Jon Lim & Evelyn Lip. *Emerald Hill Revisted.* SIA Journal. July/August. 1980.

Paul Tsakok takes the view that conservation does not mean preservation. He retains the external facade but inside the building, major structural changes have altered the spatial layering of the original.

Where the original cross wall was located, there is now a spectacular vertical space. The humble shophouse shows itself to be capable of constant adaptive reuse and internal modification.

The proportions and the quality of light are well balanced. The architect introduced a modern straight flight stair made of steel and timber with glass panels and tensioned wire. This is an interesting dialogue between the new and the old.

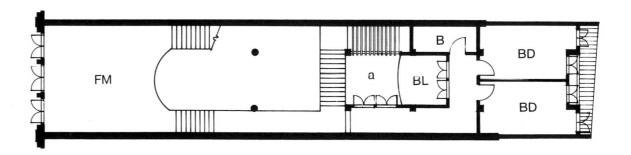

NO. 80 EMERALD HILL ROAD

Section.

Second storey plan. Two circular columns give a central emphasis to the plan.

144 **B**   Bathroom
    BD Bedroom
    BL Balcony
    D   Dining
    F   Foyer
    FM Family Room
    K   Kitchen
    L   Living

    a   airwell
    st storage

80 EMERALD HILL ROAD
SINGAPORE 0922

ARCHITECT: REGIONAL DEVELOPMENT CONSORTIUM

COMPLETED: 1988

CLIENT
Mr & Mrs Tao Hai Sin

ARCHITECT
Regional Development Consortium

PROJECT TEAM
Andrew Tan (Partner-in-charge)
Kenneth Loh (Project Architect)

CONSULTANT
Structural Engineer
Oscar Faber Consultants

MAIN CONTRACTOR
Quatre Builders Pte Ltd

One of the most influential architects in the field of conservation in recent years has been Carlo Scarpa[1]. Unrecognised outside his native Venice until the latter years of his life, he is now widely regarded as one of the most sensitive and creative architects of his generation. His best works are probably Castel Vechio in Verona and Palazzo Querina Stampadiglio in Venice. He brought to these conservation works an inspiring harmony between modern materials — steel and glass — and the ancient fabric of the buildings.

The architectural team at Regional Development Consortium has clearly gained insights from Scarpa, for there is a bold expression of modern materials in the sensitive transformation of this interior. There are other influences that one can detect in the details which do not owe their origin to the West, but are more reminiscent of the avant-garde work of Shin Takamatsu in Japan. This intriguing cocktail of source material comes together in a sparkling interior.

Two circular columns give a central emphasis to the first storey plan, and there is also a practical consideration for this arrangement. Andrew Tan, the project partner, points out that this enabled the upper floors to be supported without relying on the party walls, and also foundations could be made without costly underpinning and possible damage to adjoining property.

This structural consideration has clear repercussions on the internal space, giving it a form distinctively different to other conservation projects in Emerald Hill. The architect has also elected to form an entrance lobby, thus changing the traditional arrangement where one steps from the street into a main reception room.

The experience of the interior space is further transformed by the addition of a glazed wall around the lightwell. The effect is to flood the centre of the house with light and foreshorten the apparent length.

The quality of workmanship is all too rare, and the fact that it is carried through meticulously even to such details as the yard gate, indicates a total commitment.

The architects have revived the spirit of the former shophouse, capturing the essence of the layered space and the alternating experiences of darkness and light of the traditional layout. The lightwells, whether glazed or open, are an important part of this underlying order, and whilst RDC have moved the staircase further back than is normal, they have retained the two shafts of light — which perhaps is a little too much light.

There is an abundance of space and three bedrooms have been created, two at the second storey, while the master bedroom is in what was formerly the roof space.

The family room on the second storey is a double volume space with views out to Emerald Hill, down to the dining room, into the landscaped airwell and the reception room. There is something rather grand about the staircase which is centrally placed rather than being tucked away on a side wall. It winds around the central void and gives a theatrical setting to daily life.

The real delight of this project, however, is in the studious quality of the detailing. The intensity of thought that has gone into the design of balustrades, handrails, doors, column heads, ceilings, steel beams, arches and even the yard door testify to this fact.

Each detail is a work of modern craftsmanship. The internal lobby door and the second storey bedroom window are most delightful and closely seek inspiration from Takamatsu's unique blend of East and West. There are curious echoes of images and shapes from oriental culture transformed into steel sections and bent tubular bars. The other detail that is expressed with clarity and precision is the junction of the circular column and the transverse beam, particularly the exposed bolt heads.

Conservation will form a substantial part of the workload of Singapore architects in the next decade. This is not a result of a romantic attachment to the past but a recognition that in a society in rapid transition, it is vital to maintain continuity with its cultural heritage. RDC's solution is not a flight to pastiche, but a dialectic between modernism and tradition.

145

1. F. Dal Co and G. Mazzariol. *Carlo Scarpa — The Complete Works.* Eclecta and Architectural Press. 1987.

Two circular columns give a central emphasis to the plan — this is a practical decision which enables the upper floors to be supported without relying on the party walls. It has clear repercussions on the internal space, giving it a form which is distinctly different from the original.

The architect has shifted the focus of the house to a central axis, but he has captured the essence of the layered space of a shophouse and the alternating areas of darkness and light in the original layout.

Intense thought has gone into the details of balustrades and handrails. There is a bold expression of modern materials in the sensitive transformation of the interior.

147

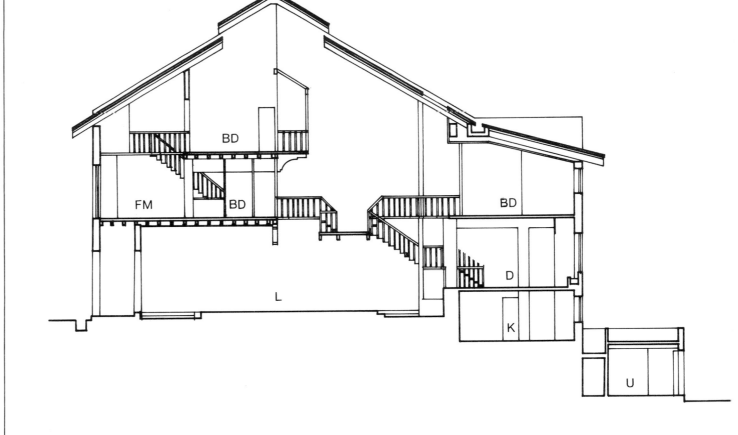

102, EMERALD HILL ROAD

Section: The three bedrooms overlook a three-storey atrium which links the activities in the house — an internal 'street'.

First storey plan. There are two internal sunken gardens — one by the main entrance, the other between the dining and living areas.

148

BD Bedrooom
D Dining
F Foyer
FM Family Room
K Kitchen
L Living
U Utility

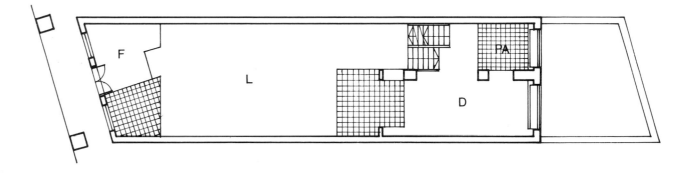

102 EMERALD HILL ROAD
SINGAPORE 0922

ARCHITECT: WILLIAM LIM ASSOCIATES

COMPLETED: 1984

CLIENT
Topham Properties Pte Ltd

ARCHITECT
William Lim Associates

PROJECT TEAM
William Lim (Partner-in-charge)
Tan Teck Kiam (Project Architect)
Leong Koh Loy (Project Manager)

CONSULTANTS
Structural Engineer
Steen Consultants Pte Ltd
Mechanical and Electrical Engineers
Steen Consultanat Pte Ltd

MAIN CONTRACTOR
Sin Heng Construction Co. Pte Ltd

Emerald Hill was the first major conservation area in Singapore. Initially the impetus for its revival came from a number of enlightened individuals and architects, Paul Tsakok and William SW Lim, who restored individual shophouses in the traditional terrace.

In 1983, the Urban Redevelopment Authority (URA) announced that the area would be preserved and set about improving the infrastructure. As momentum gathered, other individuals also acquired properties and the socio-economic profile of the area gradually changed. Given its highly desirable location close to fashionable Orchard Road, it was perhaps inevitable that the area would become 'gentrified'. This has happened elsewhere in the world and is the result of speculation as property prices rise and the area becomes an increasingly desirable place in which to live. In due course, the social structure also alters, becoming increasingly middle- to upper-income.

Whether this is desirable or not is arguable, but if market forces are given free rein, then the location is a deciding factor. It is probable that such gentrification would not occur in the Kampong Glam or Serangoon Road areas, or at least not to the same extent.

Government intervention can regulate the market to ensure the character of an area is retained, and in 1988, an extremely interesting stage in this respect was reached when Chinatown, Little India and Kampong Glam became the subjects of conservation guidelines.

No. 102 Emerald Hill is an 'act of faith' in conservation by the owners of the building. At a time when many people were sceptical about renovating old shophouses, and when the political climate was still definately pro-urban renewal, this was a case of demonstrating their conviction that the shouphouse or row house was still viable both economically and socially.

Many sceptics poured 'cold water' on such ideas, saying it did not reflect a vibrant forward-looking nation while others doubted the structural soundness of older property.

The original facade of the building has been retained, but the spatial quality of the interior is transformed. Underlying the design concept is a theme of two Malay kampong houses separated by a 'street' represented by the landing and staircase.[1]

The staircase performs a narrative function. As one ascends through the two floors of the house, a series of intriguing views are framed. One can look down into the main hall and dining area and finally, there is a spectacular view of the whole internal 'street' from the top-most rooms.

One enters the house through a hallway — a break from the traditional shophouse configuration. Indeed, it is a complete change from the same architect's design for 98 Emerald Hill Road and 2 Saunders Road. Here, the hall gives access to a vast inner room and at the rear of the first storey, the architect creates a raised area beyond an internal garden.

All the bedrooms look down into the interior of the house through open timber shutters. Balustrades behind the screens replicate the experience of looking from the interior of a traditional kampong house. The house is at its best when seen in daylight when dramatic top lighting highlights the stairs and softly penetrates the interior through the first storey windows.

The predominant colours are pale pink and natural timber; the artificial lighting subdued and mainly task-oriented. The whole feeling is of lightness and openess.

The detailing is meticulous, mostly in stained timber, exemplified in the staircase, balustrade and beams all expounding the kampong theme.

The house is intriguing but the break with the traditional layered space of a shophouse does not meet with everyone's approval. The interior is both modern and yet has cultural references. The fact that these references are Malay adds a curious paradox since shophouses are not associated with Malay dwellings. Nevertheless, it is a fine example of sensitive achitecture with implications for future directions of conservation in Singapore.

149

1. Davies, Corrine. *Female Annual '86.* pp. 195-199.

The staircase performs a narrative function. As one ascends through two floors, a series of views are framed. Underlying the design concept is the theme of two kampong houses separated by a 'street' represented by the stairwell.

From the main hall, there is a spectacular view upwards of the whole street. The predominant colours are of natural timber and pale pink. The dramatic top light highlights the interior details.

All the bedrooms look down into the interior of the house through open timber shutters. Balustrades behind the screens replicate the experience of looking from the interior of a kampong house. One former tenant said that she had wanted, from childhood, to live in a tree-house and this house gave the opportunity to do so.

The original facade of the shophouse has been retained but the spatial quality of the interior is transformed. It is a fine example of sensitive design, with implications on directions for conservation in Singapore.

151

NOS. 116,118 SOPHIA ROAD

Section. The rebuilt rear part of the house contains dining room, kitchen and bedroom. Modifications to the roof have created a clerestory window.

Plan of first storey.

152

B Bathroom
BD Bedroom
D Dining
FM Family Room
K Kitchen
L Living

a airwell
pl pool
st storage

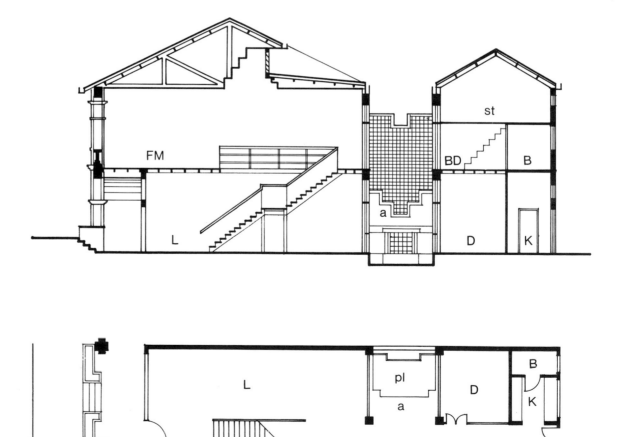

116 AND 118 SOPHIA ROAD
SINGAPORE 0922

ARCHITECT: TAG ARCHITECTS

COMPLETED: 1986

CLIENTS
Boonchai Sompolpong
Mr & Mrs Koh Guan Poh

ARCHITECT
TAG Architects

PARTNER-IN-CHARGE AND
PROJECT ARCHITECT
Boonchai Sompolpong

CONSULTANT
Structural Engineer
YF Chan Consulting Engineers

MAIN CONTRACTOR
A & B Contracts Pte. Ltd.

Mount Sophia, with its rich mixture of terrace houses and bungalows, is one of Singapore's most historically interesting areas. It still retains vestiges of its former qualities. Even today, life there seems to be just a little remote from the frantic pace of nearby Orchard Road.

Sophia Road gently ascends a hill, past some fine old buildings — the Nanyang Academy of Fine Art, the Sikh Sri Guru Singh Sabha Temple, and at the very top, a marvellous example of timber craftsmanship still survives at 12 Mount Sophia.

New commercial and residential development is gradually making inroads into the area, but just below the crest of the hill, a fine terrace of Peranakan shophouses still survives. Two of the terrace houses have been restored by Architect Boonchai Sompolpong — No. 116 for his own use, the other, No. 118, for Mr and Mrs Koh Guan Poh.

In the case of No. 116, the first storey has delightful views into the landscaped pool in the airwell. The rebuilt rear portion of the shophouse contains a bathroom, a kitchen and a dining area which also overlooks an ornamental pool.

The pool area itself is the main design intervention of the house. The architect first agreed with his neighbour to remove the solid wall between their adjacent airwells and to replace this with glass blocks. The effect is remarkable, greatly increasing the amount of light that thus floods into the adjoining rooms at first and second storey. Both houses have back-to-back waterfalls

tumbling into pools stocked with colourful Japanese carp.

The second storey has also been transformed. Structural alterations to the roof structure have created a dramatic clerestory window which floods the family living room with sunlight in the early morning. The rebuilt rear part of the house on this level contains bedrooms, bathrooms and loft space.

The architect has enhanced the old airwell of the house and introduced arched steel windows which take their cue from the geometry of the street elevation. The elevation has been lovingly restored by Boonchai Sompolpong — its ornate details being carefully cleaned and highlighted.

Classical columns, fluted pilasters, timber arched tracery, bas relief plastercasts, baroque scrolls, ornate capitals, stone balusters, eaves fretwork and ornate keystones all combine in a splendid eclectic mix, and are dominated by the

arched lintols at the first storey level.

It is slightly unfortunate that in maximising the use of the second storey the original balcony has been sacrificed. However, by keeping the new windows recessed behind the pilasters, the form of the original facade is clearly articulated.

Nos. 116 and 118 have numerous lessons for those new to restoration work, showing how the essence of the shophouse can be retained whilst making major interventions to modernise the amenities.

Their greatest success however is in recreating and enhancing the living cum working environment of the traditional shophouse. It addresses the question whether different human activities should be separated by modern zoning laws — a Western planning concept — or should the city in the tropical region reflect more traditional patterns?

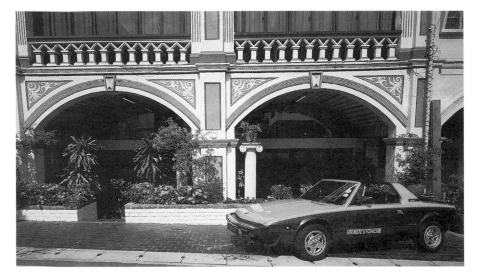

Just below the crest of Mount Sophia, a fine terrace of Peranakan shophouses survives. Two of the terrace houses have been conserved by Boonchai Sompolpong.

It is slightly unfortunate that in maximising the use of the second storey, the original balcony has been sacrificed. However, by keeping the new windows recessed behind the pilasters, the form of the original facade is clearly articulated.

The architect has lovingly restored the building's ornate details. Classical columns, fluted pilasters, timber arched tracery, bas relief plastercasts, baroque scrolls, ornate capitals, stone balusters and eaves fretwork combine in a splendid way.

The pool area is the main design intervention. The wall between the airwells of the houses has been removed and replaced with glass blocks, increasing the amount of light that floods into the rooms.

The arched steel windows around the airwell take their cue from the geometry of the balconys on the street elevation.

154

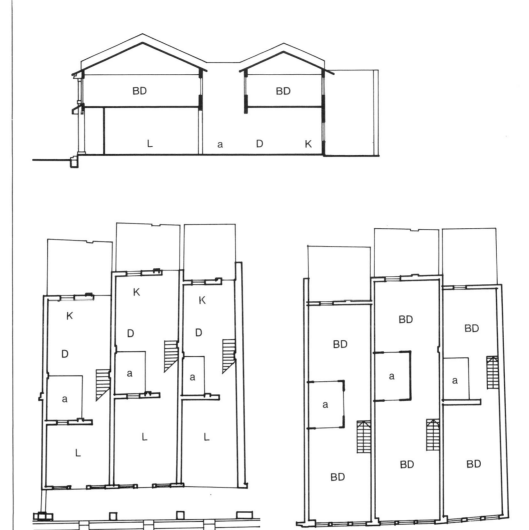

TANJONG PAGAR CONSERVATION PROJECT

This is the first major area conservation project in Singapore. It contains 220 units of two- and three-storey shophouses within 4.1 ha. in Chinatown.

First storey plan of typical units in the Tanjong Pagar Conservation area.

Second storey plan.

156

Elevation of three typical units in the conservation area.

BD Bedroom
D Dining
K Kitchen
L Living

a airwell

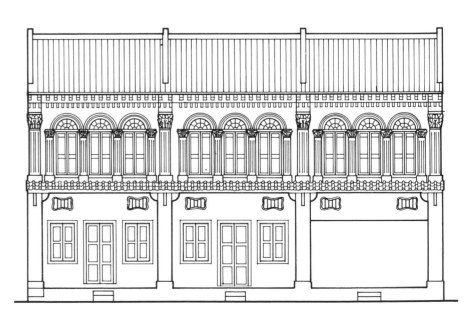

TANJONG PAGAR CONSERVATION PROJECT
NEIL ROAD, SINGAPORE 0208

ARCHITECT: URBAN REDEVELOPMENT AUTHORITY (URA)

COMPLETED: (PHASE 1) 1988

ARCHITECT
Urban Redevelopment Authority

PROJECT TEAM
Urban Redevelopment Authority

MAIN CONTRACTOR (Phase 1)
Khian Heng Construction

"There are many milestones in the history of Singapore, and this building is one of them." These were the words of Liu Thai Ker, the Chief Executive of the Housing and Development Board, when referring to No. 9 Neil Road.[1] The completion of this 'show house' as the forerunner of a major conservation project in Tanjong Pagar by the URA created a complete change of attitude to conservation in the minds of many politicians and planners in Singapore. Conservation had always been a part of the URA plans, but it is true to say that it had a low priority since the thrust of the Authority's work, until the mid-1980s, had been towards urban renewal.

Tanjong Pagar was originally developed in the 1860s and is rich in architecture and history. It has unique vernacular architecture with facade and detail designs borrowed from Chinese and Western traditions. The conservation area contains 220 units of 2- and 3-storey shophouses within 4.1 ha.

In 1981, it appeared that the area was about to give way to 'progress'. It was earmarked for public housing by the Housing and Development Board and clearance of the site was initiated.

In 1983, with the decision by the government to discontinue public housing within the city core, the URA was directed to propose alternatives. A master plan was prepared for conservation — it resulted, importantly, in the scaling down of highway proposals in the area, reassessment of plot ratios and the proposal of a central pedestrian node. Given the mood of the previous two decades, this is a major realignment of policy.

As Ilsa Sharp, a journalist, wrote vividly in June 1987: 'Singaporeans have been so well schooled in accepting that they must give way to progress, so inured to the sad sight of their elegant old buildings toppling before the bulldozer, that it would be understandable if they had gone into a state of shock on hearing the official new pro-conservation line.'

The major step forward from previous conservation projects is that this one appears to offer a new approach, building on the experience that the URA has gained from previous projects.

There is a commitment by the URA to give a lead in the conservation process. Later phases are being sold by tender to individuals. To show what can be achieved, the government has restored 32 shophouses in Phase 1.

This basically involves the re-education of a whole generation progressively estranged from its heritage by the speed of economic progress and materialism. The emergence of the first restored shophouse from half a century of grime, decay and finally neglect is truly beautiful. In the simple shophouse is a wealth of beauty and Singapore's history.

The second major advance appears to be the attempt to involve the public in the ongoing conservation. Having provided the initial impetus, it remains to be seen what the long term response will be. It also remains to be seen if the former inhabitants and trades can be attracted back, or if the area will undergo 'gentrification'. The intentions of the URA appear to be aimed at resisting this — tourists will be attracted, but hopefully only to be part of the restored indigenous way of life. The URA has encouraged a diverse mix of new tenants and owners not only to complement and enhance the Chinatown image but also to 'retain the unique ambience and character of Tanjong Pagar.'

By the time the URA stepped in with its conservation proposals, the indigenous population had already been relocated. So the attempt to recreate the former ambience will be watched with interest. In future projects, it is possible that the population could be retained and conservation go on around them with their active participation.

Conservation is relatively new in Singapore, and Tanjong Pagar is the first major area to be subject to conservation. It is a catalyst, as well as an opportunity, for Singaporean professionals and artisans to learn more about the design, implementation and management of conservation in Singapore's context.

157

1. Liu Thai Ker. *Lecture at Seminar on 'Heritage and Change in South-east Asia'*. Joint meeting of Aga Khan Program at MIT/Southeast Asia Study Group. National University of Singapore. August 1988.

In Tanjong Pagar, the Urban Renewal Authority took the decisive step of restoring 32 shophouses to provide the initial impetus for the area. The emergence of the first restored shophouse from half a century of grime is truly beautiful.

In the simple shophouse is a wealth of beauty and history. The intention of the URA is to attract a diverse mix of new tenants to complement and enhance the traditional life of Chinatown.

Tanjong Pagar has a unique vernacular architecture. Originally built in the 1860s, the facade and design were borrowed from Chinese and Western traditions.

The completion of No. 9 Neil Road as a conservation 'show house' signalled a new awareness of the value of Singapore's architectural heritage and its purpose in establishing cultural continuity.

159